HHB

HENRY DAVID THOREAU

CYCLES
AND
PSYCHE

by

Michael Sperber, MD

Celebrating **Walden** *at 150: 1854-2004*

$$\boxed{\mathcal{HHB}}$$

Higganum Hill Books : Higganum, CT

3-20-2006
LAN
$17.95

First Edition
First Printing, September 1, 2004

Higganum Hill Books
P.O. Box 666, Higganum, Connecticut 06441-0666
Phone: (860) 345-4103
Email: rcdebold@mindspring.com

Edited by Randall Conrad / The Thoreau Project
<www.calliope.org/thoreau/>

Library of Congress Control Number 2004009222
ISBN: 0-9741158-2-7

Cover Daguerreotype of Henry David Thoreau, age 39
By permission of The Thoreau Society, Lincoln, Mass.

Library of Congress Cataloging-in-Publication Data

Sperber, Michael, 1931-
  Henry David Thoreau : cycles and psyche / by Michael Sperber.
    p. cm.
  ISBN 0-9741158-2-7 (alk. paper)
  1. Thoreau, Henry David, 1817-1862--Psychology. 2. Authors,
American--19th century--Psychology. 3. Authorship--Psychological
aspects. 4. Psychology and literature. I. Title.
  PS3053.S68 2004
  818'.309--dc22

                                    2004009222

Printed in the United States of America
Higganum Hill Books is distributed by Independent Publishers Group:
Phone: (800) 888-4741 <ipgbook.com>

Contents

...to

Lisa

Jeff

Skip

and

Schatzie

Preface

I

Henry David Thoreau (1817-1862), arguably America's supreme and certainly its most original genius, was incarcerated for one July night in 1846 at virtually the same penal institution where I work today as a psychiatric consultant.* Thoreau, an abolitionist, had refused to pay his poll tax, which he said would support inhuman and immoral laws: *"Under a government which imprisons any unjustly, the true place for a just man is also a prison."*

Had he further been overheard declaiming against the Fugitive Slave Law, as he did 150 years ago to a large crowd, *"My thoughts are murder to the State, and involuntarily go plotting against her,"* Thoreau's path would cross mine, according to current practices.

Like the rest of Thoreau's community at the time, the influential philosopher Ralph Waldo Emerson considered his friend Thoreau's act of civil disobedience "mean and skulking." No one imagined that Thoreau's twenty-some-page record of that remarkable act would one day affect millions who would struggle for their freedom under the leadership of Mohandas K. Gandhi and Dr. Martin Luther King, Jr.

Personally, I admire those who act from principle (depending on the principle, of course), and who practice what they preach (not always the case with Emerson).

Ignoring my personal beliefs, a referral from the Sheriff's Department would request only my professional opinion of this man Thoreau. Specifically, would he pose a substantial risk of harm to himself or others by reason of insanity, requiring involuntary

---

* The equivalent lockup is part of the Middlesex Sheriff's Office elsewhere, although today's Concord contains a prison on its far outskirts.

psychiatric hospitalization?**

A complicated question ! Thoreau, who coped heroically with severe mood, stress, and personality disorders, diagnosed himself on at least one occasion as having recurrent "Insanity." Nor was Thoreau a confirmed pacifist, despite the popular misconception.

It will become clear to readers of this book that although Thoreau had episodes of severe emotional disorder, he politicized that mental anguish, using it constructively. Thoreau was among *"the lovers of law and order,"* as he wrote, *"who observe the law when the government breaks it."* Far from being a menace to himself and others by reason of mental illness, he was an effective force in promoting his own mental health and that of society collectively.

II

This book would never have been written had it not been for two questions, posed a decade and a half apart by two gifted teachers, thoughtful men and great souls: Professors Henry A. Murray and Walter Harding. Murray as a literary scholar blazed new trails in the study of Herman Melville; as a psychologist at Harvard he originated in the 1930s the widely used Thematic Apperception Test, and described the "Icarus complex" in 1955. I used that concept as the framework for an essay on Albert Camus's 1956 novel of alienation, *The Fall.* By the time Murray accepted my paper for publication in *American Imago*, the Icarus complex was well established in psychology. Now Murray wondered if its expression in modern literature could help elucidate a fuller clinical understanding of its etiology. As we discussed Camus's anti-hero, Clamence, he caught me off guard with his question: "What finally underlies all these Icarian traits of his? Have you formed any idea?"

That was in 1966. I discovered my answer only in 1982, when a chain of events led me to Walter Harding, the pre-eminent Thoreau expert of his generation.

** Thoreau's Middlesex County, needless to remark, had no such thing as a psychiatric facility for the criminally insane.

I should explain that after living with my young children in shacks smaller than Thoreau's for longer periods than Thoreau, on the dune wilderness of Cape Cod and on the island of St. Lucia, West Indies, I had absorbed the salubrious effect of a Thoreauvian lifestyle that combined natural simplicity with self-reform. So, following my appointment as psychiatrist on the "Concord Unit" of the now defunct Metropolitan State Hospital, I had changed its name to the "Thoreau Unit."

It occurred to me that the Thoreau Society, always collecting bits of news, would be curious to hear about the new eponym. I received a cordial reply from Harding himself, asking if I would do a presentation at the annual members' gathering in Concord. In the talk I gave, "Thoreau and Mental Health," I discussed the importance of such Thoreauvian practices as self-reform, journal-keeping, adopting a challenge orientation toward life, living simply and naturally, moral commitment, and finding one's inner center from which to control one's problems.

After the meeting, Walt took me aside and disclosed a gap in his understanding. "I've collected Thoreau's dreams," he said, "but I have no more clue than the dreamer about their meaning." He asked me if twentieth-century psychiatry could cast light upon them. (He had put together a conference several years earlier, "Psychology and the Literary Artist" – namely Thoreau – and now a collection of the participants' essays was being readied for publication. The book, *Thoreau's Psychology,* edited by Raymond Gozzi, came out the following year.)

We met regularly for a couple of summers in the little house behind Concord's First Parish Church, spurred on by Thoreau's contention in his journal that *"the nearest approach to discovering what we are is in dreams."* Walt provided me with the dreams and the journal entries for context (and a copy of his landmark biography *The Days of Henry Thoreau,* just republished), while I attempted to correlate Thoreau's "days" with his nocturnal visions.

By the time we came to Thoreau's recurrent childhood

"Rough-Smooth" nightmare – which he declared was like his life, *"an alternate … Insanity and Sanity"* – it was clear to me that Thoreau had suffered from severe bipolar ("manic-depressive") disorder from his early years.

What is more, I encountered many forms of "high-flying" imagery associated with Murray's Icarus complex in the sketches, recurring dreams, hallucinations and literary imaginings of Thoreau during his bouts with mania. Correspondingly, the prevalent imagery during episodes of depression was subterranean and circuitous, and so I began to call them Daedalian. I reported the results of my findings to the Thoreau Society in 1985 in a talk, "Thoreau's Recurrent Dreams," which became Chapter 4 of the present monograph.

III

Although the term "psychobiography" will inevitably be applied to this book, the word is a misnomer. Any book by that name is a highly detailed, full-length life story, framed by a particular psychological viewpoint and marshaling substantial evidence to support its assertions. Richard Lebeaux's painstaking Eriksonian volumes, *Young Man Thoreau* and *Thoreau's Seasons,* are excellent cases in point.

The present work considers much the same themes as Lebeaux – Thoreau's traumatic losses, mood swings and search for identity – but it does so from a psychiatric perspective. It is obviously not a full-length biography, but instead focuses in some clinical detail upon Thoreau's symptoms of severe mood, stress, and personality disorders – and on his self-therapeutic successes.

I offer this book as a modest contribution to research in psychiatry and creative expression. It is hoped that, just as Oedipus comes to mind when a struggle exists between father and son for the affections of the woman in their lives, so the story of Icarus and Daedalus will prove useful in illuminating certain types of mood disorders. Recognition of imagery associated with these archetypes could be of great value as a diagnostic tool for the identification of underlying hypomania, mania, depression, dysthymia, cyclothymia and bipolar (manic-depressive) disorder.

IV

Having found answers to the leading questions of my mentors, I assembled the material for the present study after a long gestation. For their irreplaceable help, I express heartfelt appreciation to the colleagues, friends and family who have supported my efforts.

Randall Conrad drew upon extensive knowledge of the field in performing diligent editorial work. His good-humored, painstaking attention to detail during our ongoing dialogues demonstrated a truly Thoreauvian spirit. Many of this book's strengths result from his expertise. I assume all responsibility for any shortcomings.

Doug Worth, who read and commented on versions of this work, has been a devoted and supportive friend, soul-ally and literary mentor. Thanks to him, I met Dr. Richard DeBold, founder and editor-in-chief of Higganum Hill Books.

Dick not only steered *Henry David Thoreau: Cycles and Psyche* through the demanding cycles of publication requirements and deadlines with the confidence and skill of long experience, but also wrought an ingenious cover design based on the familiar daguerreotype taken of Thoreau at age 39. That portrait expresses the effect Emerson felt in Thoreau's gaze: "He understood at a glance, and saw the limitations and poverty of those he talked with, so that nothing seemed concealed from such terrible eyes." Dick's "doppelgänger" layout captures this book's *raison d'être* – to peer behind those terrible eyes.

My warm appreciation goes to the Thoreau Society and to those members who shared their expertise to make this a better book. I am grateful in particular to the Society's Executive Director, Jayne Gordon, for the opportunity to return to Walt Harding's podium for a third time at the 2004 members' gathering in Concord. I owe a debt of gratitude to Elizabeth Hall Witherell, Editor-in-Chief of *The Writings of Henry D. Thoreau,* for illuminating discussions ranging from mind, brain and body to hypergraphia and penmanship in the nineteenth century. Marilyn Palmeri, manager of photography and rights at the Pierpont Morgan Library, fitted her colleagues in Literary and Historic Manuscripts with talaria.

Special thanks to Dr. Bruce Price, Chief of Neurology at McLean Hospital, for reviewing a section of the manuscript.

Rosalie Prosser and her team at Alice Darling Secretarial Services have been extremely patient and helpful in keeping up with my hypergraphia over the years, deciphering often illegible handwriting. Karen Packard, artful manager of the Wales Copy Center division of Andrew T. Johnson Co., resolved eleventh-hour technical snarls with graceful efficiency.

Among my debts of a more personal nature, I express gratitude to my daughter Lisa and son Jeff, who in their early years shared with me the wildernesses on the North and South Atlantic shores. Adults now, they share with me their lives of simplicity, independence, magnanimity, and trust – attributes of wisdom, according to Thoreau.

My brother Skip has been the sort of father-figure to me that John Thoreau Jr. was to Henry. Caring and thoughtful, he always brings a good idea to share, new shingles for us to whittle.

When I washed ashore, shipwrecked in Belgium, more than four decades ago, Claude Bloch helped me to survive, and has been a loyal, patient, steadfast friend and ego-ideal ever since.

Schatzie, compassionate and unpretentious, aligns her soul with nature, making it fruitful, bringing forth imagination. Rarest of treasures, she is the woman of my dreams.

Michael Allen Sperber

Peaked Hill Dunes, Cape Cod, Mass., 1974,

Cambridge, Mass., 2004

Henry David Thoreau

CYCLES

AND

PSYCHE

Introduction

Mysteries and Revelations

I

Apsychiatrist writing about Henry David Thoreau is blessed and cursed by the subject's literary legacy. The curse is Thoreau's guarded nature. *"For an impenetrable shield,"* he wrote, *"stand inside yourself."* (1:106) Joyce Carol Oates, no stranger to complex, enigmatic characters, put it well: "Of our classic American writers Henry David Thoreau is the supreme poet of doubleness, of evasion and mystery. Who is he? Where does he stand?" [1] This study explores Thoreau's psychological vulnerabilities – chiefly guilt, shame, and an abhorrence of being judged – which led to his impervious defenses.

Another of Thoreau's curses is a blessing. Hypergraphia was one symptom of the manic phase of his severe bipolar disorder (Chapter 4), and at such times could be revealing. Consider his self-diagnosis of "Insanity," which he confided to his journal at the age of 39, on the fifteenth anniversary of his beloved older brother's tragic, shocking death from lockjaw. (Mania can be a defense against underlying depression.) After describing, in vivid tactile terms, a recurrent dream that plagued him in childhood – "Rough" nightmares alternating with "Smooth" dreams of bliss – Thoreau adds, almost as an afterthought: *"My waking experience always has been and is such an alternate Rough and Smooth. In other words it is Insanity and Sanity."* (9:210-11; Thoreau's emphasis.)

There are other revelations. Thoreau's journal, begun in the fall of 1837 and continued until two months before his death in 1862 at age 44, provides a window on his mental processes, especially in the earlier years before he had any inkling that these volumes might some day be published. In it, we can trace

Thoreau's mood swings over the years (Chapters 4-9) and the imagery he used to describe them. It is hypothesized in this study that Icarian imagery (defined in Chapter 7) corresponds to underlying mania, Daedalian (Chapter 8) to depression.

Also depicted in the journal is the enormous mountain which Thoreau repeatedly hallucinated (Chapter 3), imagining that it sat upon Concord's real-life "Burying-Hill," in which his brother was interred. Was the mountain a symbolic tombstone in honor of Thoreau's ego-ideal?

Among other mysteries, Thoreau developed facsimile lockjaw, a near-fatal conversion disorder, eleven days after his brother died of the actual disease (Chapter 1). Was this psychosomatic disorder an expression of his "as-if" personality (Chapter 11)?

II

Thoreau was a great man, and this presents another problem specifically because, as he came to understand in his relationship with Emerson (and recognized in himself): *"Great persons are not soon learned, not even in their outlines, but they change like mountains in the horizon as we ride along."* (1:437)

Given this complexity, mysterious nature, and greatness, Thoreau is not easily grasped psychologically, although some excellent psychological studies published in the later twentieth century pioneered new perspectives. Each focuses on Thoreau's multifaceted psyche from its own perspective. Taken together, they allow a synoptic view.

The Freudian account, Raymond Gozzi's *Tropes and Figures: A Psychoanalytic Study of David Henry Thoreau* (1957), emphasizes the impact of Thoreau's early years on his life and work, making it the first book-length study of Thoreau to use the tools of depth psychology. [2]

Richard   Lebeaux's   well-researched,   two-volume Eriksonian analysis *(Young Man Thoreau,* 1977, and *Thoreau's Seasons,* 1984) considers the formative experiences of early trauma and loss, and chronicles the way subsequent crises continued to shape the "seasons" of his life, his adult development and creative writings.

Henry David Thoreau: Cycles and Psyche introduces into Thoreau studies, for the first time, a psychiatric perspective, which I hope will help elucidate the mysteries and revelations of Thoreau's serious stress, mood, and personality disorders – acute facsimile lockjaw and chronic post-traumatic stress, bipolar, and "as-if" personality disorders.

This book not only documents psychopathology, but also describes the innovative, self-reliant methods Thoreau devised to achieve and maintain mental equilibrium in the face of these severe emotional disturbances (Chapters 13-16).

Thoreau's unfinished project during his last years, which he sometimes called (and spelled) his "Kalendar" (Chapter 14), provides a good example of these innovative strategies. Compiling the data he had recorded in more than ten years' observations in Concord's woodlands, he began to construct a phenological chart or *"calendar of the seasons." "The seasons and all their changes are in me,"* he understood. *"After a while I learn what my moods and seasons are."* (10:127) This knowledge enabled Thoreau to predict and control them more effectively than he could in his youth.

We readily think of Thoreau's enormous contributions to world literature, moral philosophy, political theory, and environmental science. How often do we consider his contributions to good mental health?

III

I would here like to introduce readers to many other attributes of Thoreau's, neither mysterious nor revelatory, that I find admirable, but I will confine myself to two – enough is as good as a feast.

Despite the mental afflictions from which Thoreau suffered beginning in childhood, and tuberculosis probably from his college years, he maintained a positive attitude. *"Surely joy is the condition of life,"* he believed. [3] Although Thoreau was severely depressed at times, it was never for long. This is no mystery, for

Thoreau was challenge-oriented. Whatever did not destroy him, he believed, would contribute to his strengths.

Self-reform was the keystone of Thoreau's self-healing:

> *If, then, we would indeed restore mankind by truly Indian, botanic, magnetic or natural means, let us first be as simple and well as Nature ourselves, dispel the clouds which hang over our own brows, and take up a little life into our pores.* [4]

And there is no need to delay. *"The true reform can be undertaken any morning before unbarring our doors,"* Thoreau wrote when he was 23. *"I can do two thirds the reform of the world myself."* (1:247)

Our over-medicated society, with its frayed nerves, emotional disequilibrium, unreason and hostilities, is ready for Thoreau's self-reform. "Society is more benefited by one sincere life, by seeing how one man helped himself, than by all the other projects that human policy has devised for their salvation," wrote another transcendental philosopher, Frederic Henry Hedge. If it applies to anyone in our season, certainly that one is Henry David Thoreau. [5]

Prologue

A Lovely Lady and a Man-Weathercock

Thoreau described an outing with the object of his affection in his journal on June 19, 1840, evoking a clear-sighted Icarian freedom (floating on water, gazing skyward) that is sadly clouded by human turpitude:

> *The other day I rowed in my boat a free, even lovely young lady, and, as I plied the oars, she sat in the stern, and there was nothing but she between me and the sky. So might all our lives be picturesque if they were free enough, but mean relations and prejudices intervene to shut out the sky, and we never see a man as simple and clearly as the man-weathercock on a steeple.* (1:144) [1]

The young lady was Ellen Sewall, a 17-year-old beauty from out of town, and Thoreau was courting her during one of her visits to the Thoreau household, where her aunt and grandmother were longtime boarders.

It is puzzling that Thoreau began his journal entry gazing at this lovely maiden, and ended with a view of a *"man-weathercock on a steeple."*

The entry is less perplexing when we sort out the order of events taking place during the all-important summer of 1839. The attractive Ellen, who first appeared on the Thoreau doorstep in July, had been preceded by another, younger Sewall who cast a similar spell over Henry.

This was her 11-year-old brother Edmund, who arrived in Concord in June to visit the same relatives. (The following year, Edmund would be enrolled in the private school run by Henry and his brother John.) Almost immediately, Henry composed the homoerotic poem, "Sympathy," in homage to the youngster:

Lately alas I knew a gentle boy.

...

On every side he open was as day.

...

In other sense this youth was glorious,
Himself a kingdom wheresoe'er he came.

...

So was I taken unawares by this,
I quite forgot my homage to confess;
Yet now am forced to know, though hard it is,
I might have loved him, had I loved him less.

Each moment, as we nearer drew to each,
A stern respect withheld us farther yet,
So that we seemed beyond each other's reach,
And less acquainted than when first we met. ... [2]

Touching as it does upon the core question of Thoreau's sexuality, "Sympathy" is usually Exhibit A in biographers' discussions of his homoeroticism. *

One month after Edmund's arrival, his older sister Ellen made her appearance in Thoreau's erotically awakened life. It has been stated that Thoreau "immediately forgot" about Edmund as a consequence. [3] From a psychological standpoint, however, it is far more likely that Thoreau retained his indelible impression of the *"gentle boy,"* now repressed to a subconscious level. Thus, it is possible to interpret Thoreau's rowing passage as follows.

Facing Ellen as he plied the oars, bi-erotic Thoreau may have had fantasies about her brother, whom he would have liked to see as *"simple and distinct as the man-weathercock."* In reality, then, what intervened to *"shut out the sky"* (or to muddy Thoreau's *"simple and distinct"* vision of Edmund) was not *"mean relations and prejudices,"*

---

* Thoreau's sexual orientation – discussed further in Chapters 6 and 12 – was researched only in the later twentieth century. From the evidence, he was homosexually inclined, yet celibate all his life. (Harding, "Thoreau's Sexuality," 39-40.)

but the love-object who had unseated him, the pleasantly disturbing Ellen.

An alternative interpretation is that the *"mean relations and prejudices"* that intruded to *"shut out the sky"* could be attributed to Ralph Waldo Emerson, Thoreau's mentor. The older man had been disturbed enough by the poem to try to cover up its implications, insisting that Henry had written it about Ellen, not Edmund. [4]

A Romantic Triangle

Another conflict introduced further complications. When Ellen visited the Thoreau family in July, 1839, John Jr. fell in love with her at the same time as Henry. As a result, the rivalry between Thoreau and his older brother, usually subliminal, came to the fore. Further, it has been hypothesized that Thoreau unconsciously initiated the romantic triangle of 1839. Perhaps Henry was seeking not so much to win Ellen as to hold on to John, whom he feared to lose, by thwarting his attention to Ellen. [5]

That fall, the brothers took a rowboat journey up the Concord and Merrimack Rivers into New Hampshire and back, which was to become the subject of Thoreau's first book-length publication, *A Week on the Concord and Merrimack Rivers*, ten years later. As we shall discuss in the next chapter, Henry's book became a memorial to John, who died less than three years after the excursion.

In his journal entry for June 19, 1840, after reporting the boat ride with Ellen, Thoreau noted that he heard faint bugle notes, the *"friendly"* lowing of cows, and the whippoorwill's call in the distance. It was, he writes, *"the voice with which the woods and moonlight woo me."* He then formed an association between this and the river excursion with John, which had had a similar auditory ambience: *"I shall not soon forget the sounds which lulled me when falling asleep on the banks of the Merrimack."* (1:144) He described the sounds he heard as the brothers camped near Penichook Brook:

*Far into the night I hear some tyro beating a drum
incessantly with a view to some country muster, and am
thrilled by an infinite sweetness as of a music which the
breeze drew from the sinews of war. ... I see fields where no
hero couched his lance.* (1:145) *

---

* Thoreau used this incessant drummer in *A Week* ("Monday," 173.) The
faraway figure evolved into the often-cited *"different drummer,"* eleven years
later. (*Walden*, "Conclusion," 326.)

1

Facsimile Lockjaw

Mirroring a Sardonic Grin

On New Year's Day, 1842, Henry's beloved older brother, John Thoreau, Jr., sliced off the tip of his ring finger while stropping his razor. He replaced the severed piece, staunched the flow of blood with a cloth, and bandaged the wound.

A few days later, he began experiencing pain. On January 8, he removed the bandage, noticed that the adhered skin was "mortified," and went to a doctor who merely redressed the wound. As he made his way home, John's physical distress became intense. By morning, trismus – the tetanic spasm causing rigid closure of the jaws ("lockjaw") – set in.

Tetanus is a disease of the nervous system characterized by intense activity of motor neurons resulting in severe spasms. It is caused by *Clostridium tetani*, an anaerobic, gram positive, spore-forming rod. In the presence of anaerobic conditions, the spores germinate. With microbial autolysis, tetanospasmin, one of the most powerful neurotoxins known, is released. The toxin attacks synaptic functioning by causing disinhibition; generalized muscle rigidity results, leading to trismus, *risus sardonicus* (a sneering expression), laryngospasm, opisthotonus, dysphagia, and tonic contraction of respiratory muscles preventing adequate respiration. Hypoxia causes irreversible CNS damage and death.

In those days before antiserum, there was nothing to do but watch and wait. A physician called in from Boston was candid: in this, his twenty-seventh year, John would die a painful but speedy death. A contemporary recorded John's "unmoved" reaction in these words:

"Is there no hope?" he said. "None," replied the doctor. Then, although his friends were almost distracted around him, he was calm, saying, "The cup that my father gives me, shall I not drink it?" He bade his friends all good-by... He died Tuesday [January 11], at two o'clock, P.M., with as much cheerfulness and composure of mind as if only going a short journey. [1]

On the day of John's death, Lidian (Mrs. Ralph Waldo) Emerson, who knew the Thoreau brothers well, wrote:

After J. had taken leave of all the family he said to Henry now sit down and talk to me of Nature and Poetry, I shall be a good listener for it is difficult for me to interrupt you. During the hour in which he died, he looked at Henry with a 'transcendent smile full of Heaven' (I think this was H's expression) and Henry 'found himself returning it' and this was the last communication that passed between them. [2]

These benign depictions do not convey the ghastly nature of death from tetanus: suffocation due to paralysis of the respiratory muscles, the jaws locked and the lips drawn back in a "sardonic grin" *(risus sardonicus)* from facial-musculature spasms. Once we fathom the dreadful nature of John's death, we grasp the severity of Henry's subsequent stress disorder.

John was the only person in Henry's life whom he loved, admired and trusted. Henry, a devoted and attentive caretaker throughout the illness, held him in his arms when he died.

On January 22, eleven days later, Henry also developed symptoms of lockjaw. Doctors were afraid he, too, would die, even though there were no skin breaks for *Clostridium tetani* to lodge, exsporulate, and release their deadly neurotoxin. On the 24th, Henry took a turn for the better, and in the weeks that followed, he gradually recovered from what would today be called facsimile lockjaw, a form of psychosomatic conversion disorder.

The concept of conversion disorder was one of Freud's earliest contributions to medical psychology. Freud hypothesized two avenues by which the patient might discharge unbearably painful affect – either its conversion into physical symptoms, or its displacement into obsessions, compulsions and phobias. It is, in other words, a mental condition that mimics a physical illness. [3]

Thoreau's grief-connected facsimile lockjaw occurred through identification with, and imitation of, his brother.* Becoming the moribund "other" bypasses the normal stages of grieving.

Being afflicted by – and almost dying from – the same disease may also have helped Thoreau atone for heavy guilt that he felt.

Sibling Rivalry and Oedipal Guilt

To grasp the Thoreau brothers' relationship and the source of Henry's guilt feelings, we must go back in time. Their father, John Thoreau, Sr., has been described as a "mousy sort of man," little involved in the activities of his gifted sons. John, Jr., in contrast, was said to be "saintly minded, ... a bright spot everywhere; the life of every gathering." John not only was a loving brother but also frequently served as a father to Henry. They spent much time together in nature. John had a gift for finding Indian arrowheads along the ground, and showed Henry where to look for them. They had mock-Indian names for each other. John taught Henry how to recognize birds by their calls and trees by their leaves. As young men the brothers taught together in the private school they ran for two years, teaching the youngsters to learn by doing – progressive education. [4]

As we have seen, both brothers fell in love with Ellen in 1839, when John was 24 and Henry 22. Upon returning home from their excursion on the Concord and Merrimack Rivers, and

---

* Imitation is the mode by which those with an "as-if" personality (described in Chapter 11) relate to others.

during the subsequent year, John and Henry became rival suitors. Possibly the brothers' unspoken rivalry became explicit during the excursion. [5]

Henry passively deferred to the older brother, who proposed marriage almost as soon as he was back from the river trip; Henry waited anxiously to learn the result. After some indecision, Ellen turned John down. When Henry subsequently proposed by letter, Ellen declined his offer too. Following John's death, survival guilt must have mingled in Henry's psyche with guilt over this all-but-acknowledged rivalry, complicating the process of grieving and mourning.

Another sudden loss in Thoreau's "family" occurred about the same time, intensifying Thoreau's stress disorder. On January 25, just as Thoreau was beginning to recover from facsimile lockjaw, Emerson's five-year-old son Waldo died suddenly of scarlet fever. During his stays at the Emerson' home, Thoreau had developed a particular affection for Waldo, whom he considered *"a boy of rare promise."* Above all, the child's death brought Thoreau even closer to the grief-wracked Emerson, perhaps further strengthening his "as-if" identification with his mentor and father-figure. [6]

A third loss one year later may have reinforced Thoreau's stresses at the same time that it helped him visualize the "wilderness therapy" which would later help him. Charles Stearns Wheeler, a Harvard classmate, died from "gastric fever" at 26, in Germany, where he had been studying. Thoreau had once camped during a summer vacation at Wheeler's cabin on a local pond, an experience thought to have helped inspire the famous Walden retreat.

Post-Traumatic Stress: Aftermath

Following recovery from the near-fatal facsimile lockjaw, and suffering from post-traumatic stress disorder (PTSD, Chapter 2), Thoreau, still depressed, moved back in with the Emerson family, where he had been living and writing while Ralph Waldo Emerson paid him for work as a handyman. Emerson, his mentor of several years, found him a position on Staten Island, New York, as a tutor to his nephews, but Thoreau developed hypersomnia (sleep disturbances are common in stress disorders), felt homesick for the poplars in his Concord backyard, and had to return early.

Denial was one way for Thoreau to cope with his overwhelming loss. Not long after the death, Thoreau had written in his journal that the *"sad memory of departed friends is soon incrusted over with sublime and pleasing thoughts,"* that nature heals every wound, and *"presents nothing in a state of death"* (1:328). The latter insight would become a cornerstone of Thoreau's philosophy. (See Chapter 7, "Desire for Immortality.")

Back home, on the last day of April 1844, Thoreau and a friend inadvertently set fire to 300 acres of privately owned Concord woodland. This troublesome experience is discussed in Chapter 7. Thoreau was as fascinated by the blaze as Icarus by the sun. But (although he could never bring himself to say it aloud) he was also remorseful. Thoreau returned to the fire more than once in his journal, trying to get both the guilt and the delight written out. This was his therapy, turning chagrins into a song through the art of writing – reworking his psyche's "ode to dejection" until he could *"brag as lustily as chanticleer in the morning."* (See Chapter 15, "Writing it Out.") [7]

Distractedness is symptomatic of PTSD. The young naturalist's surprising inattention to the presence of highly combustible dry vegetation near his cooking-fire was most likely due to preoccupation with guilt and grief over John. Building the fire in the vicinity of Fair Haven, the Thoreau brothers' favorite haunt, undoubtedly contributed to Henry's difficulties concentrating. [8]

"Some Private Business to Transact"

Thoreau acted from principles, and it troubled him that he could not explain two of the most important actions in his life.

On July 4, 1845, he began living at Walden Pond, on the outskirts of Concord, in a one-room house he had built himself.

He returned two years, two months, and two days later, to become *"a sojourner in civilized life again."* [9]

Unclear about his reason for going to Walden, Thoreau searched for an explanation and articulated a courageous and resonant, albeit psychologically superficial, formulation: *"I went to the woods because I wished to live deliberately, to front only the essential facts of life, and see if I could not learn what it had to teach, and not, when I came to die, discover that I had not lived."* [10]

Thoreau's reason for leaving was just as vague: *"I left the woods for as good a reason as I went there,"* he writes in *Walden's* conclusion. *"Perhaps it seemed to me that I had several more lives to live, and could not spare any more time for that one."* [11]

Earlier in the same book Thoreau revealed that there was a reason, but one he found too personal to disclose: *"My purpose in going to Walden Pond was not to live cheaply nor to live dearly there, but to transact some private business with the fewest obstacles."* [12]

That private business – his writing project in the woods of Walden – was Thoreau's effort to lift a heavy weight from his shoulders. In his pond-side retreat, writing of the boating and walking excursion he and John had once taken together, he became aware that *"...like some Indian tribes, we bear about with us the mouldering relics of our ancestors on our shoulders."* [13]

Writing out his grief by drafting *A Week on the Concord and Merrimack Rivers* while at Walden did not completely remove the mouldering ancestral relics from Thoreau's shoulders. An elegy, unlike a dirge, is a rather constrictive form. The deceased is never mentioned by name, and it is not really possible to grieve an unnamed corpse.

In *A Week*, Thoreau's prose elegy for his brother, a core theme appears in a quoted saying of the Chinese Confucian philosopher Mencius: "The duties of practical philosophy consist only in seeking after those sentiments of the heart which we have lost; that is all." It could be said that *A Week on the Concord and Merrimack Rivers*, like the remainder of Thoreau's life, was an exercise in practical philosophy. [14]

2

Post-Traumatic Stress Disorder

The grotesque, shocking, unexpected death of the best friend Thoreau would ever have, aggravated by the deaths of two other people important to his life, was devastating to his psyche. Thoreau suffered what is commonly called a "nervous breakdown," or in psychiatric parlance, an episode of post-traumatic stress disorder (PTSD). *"Each such experience,"* he would later write, *"is an assault on our vital force."* (11:438)

This syndrome commonly includes the following characteristics:

1. **Psychic numbing** (emotional anesthesia).
2. **Hypervigilance**: the senses on high alert.
3. **Cognitive disturbances**: nightmares, daydreams, flashbacks, and distractibility.
4. **Anniversary phenomena**: reactivation of original symptoms or psychological associations on anniversaries of the trauma.

In all these respects, Thoreau experienced PTSD.

1. Psychic Numbing

Psychic numbing (emotional anesthesia) results from the withdrawal of emotional energy from life, especially those aspects of life connected with the trauma. Thoreau described this *"deadening"* in a journal entry written on the day his father died:

I perceive that we partially die ourselves through sympathy at the death of each of our friends or near relatives. ... It becomes a source of wonder that they who have lost many friends still live. After long watching around the sick-bed of a friend, we, too, partially give up the ghost with him, and are the less to be identified with this state of things. (11:438)

This passage may also be the expression of Thoreau's "as-if" imitative mode (Chapter 11).

2. Hypervigilance

Whether alone in the woodlands or negotiating Concord's Main Street (depicted in *Walden* as a gantlet of aggressive, practically assaultive commerce) – whether to open himself to healing nature or to protect himself from societal toxins – Thoreau perpetually kept his acute hearing, keen eyesight, and indeed all his sensory and intellectual faculties on high alert. His tense bearing and clenched hands, his frequent self-identification as a soldier, and his oppositional defiance in debate or discussion are powerful evidence of the need Thoreau felt to be wary of the enemy, to defend himself against the world. [1]

3. Cognitive Disturbances

Expressions of cognitive disturbances are found in the letter of April 10, 1853, and the journal entry of September 24, 1859, both discussed in the concluding sections of Chapter 4. In each instance, the stream of associations and flight of ideas obscure the typical clarity of Thoreau's prose, making its allusions and connections virtually impossible for a reader to decipher.

4. Anniversary Phenomena

In a journal entry composed only five days after John's death, Thoreau expresses both the pain of abandonment and the psychic numbing that anesthetizes against it. He identifies himself as the victim of a nerve disease like that which took John from him, and denies all worth to his own life, picturing himself as a corpse, the living dead:

> *What am I at present? A diseased bundle of nerves standing between time and eternity like a withered leaf that still hangs shivering on its stem. A more miserable object one could not well imagine – but still very dull very insipid to think of. I suppose I may live on not a few years – trailing this carcass after me –or perhaps trailing after it...* [2]

As foreseen, Thoreau's life did continue without John for more than *"a few years,"* and on many subsequent Januaries he experienced recurrent depression with recollections of the wrenching loss that had left him a diseased bundle of nerves. These anniversaries were all the more painful because Thoreau was apparently most often unconscious of the reason for his miserable feelings.

One anniversary – the eleventh – coincided with a deadly explosion at a gunpowder factory in the next town, to which Thoreau experienced a variety of emotional responses after viewing the aftermath in person. Psychic numbing is evident in the depersonalized style of his immediate journal description:

> *Some of the clothes of the men were in the tops of the trees, where undoubtedly their bodies had been and left them. The bodies were naked and black, some limbs and bowels here and there, and a head at a distance from its trunk. The feet were bare; the hair singed to a crisp. I smelt the powder half a mile before I got there. Put the different buildings thirty rods apart, and then but one will blow up at a time.* (4:455)

The hair-raising proximity of sudden death undoubtedly reactivated emotional conflicts over his brother, or feelings about men working with gunpowder:

> *Day before yesterday I looked at the mangled and*
> *blackened bodies of men which had been blown up by*
> *powder, and felt that the lives of men were not innocent, and*
> *that there was an avenging power in nature. (4:459)*

Two weeks after viewing the grisly remains of the explosion victims, Thoreau had a nightmare connected to the experience: *"I dreamed of delving amid the graves of the dead."* The "deadening" he had felt several days after John's death recurred: *"Death is with me, and life far away."* (4:472) Thoughts of death recurred quite often during the stressful, emotionally laden year of 1853. [3]

Distractedness, part of the PTSD syndrome, is apparent five days later:

> *Made a roaring fire on the edge of the meadow ... I burnt*
> *off my eyelashes when the fire suddenly blazed up with the*
> *wind, without knowing that I had come very near it.*

Icarian absorption with the flame (Chapter 7) is evident:

> *We chose a place which afforded a prospect, but it turned*
> *out we looked only at the fire. It made all places indifferent.*
> *The color of the coals, in a glowing heap or seen through the*
> *white ashes on the brands, like rubies. (4:479)*

On the fifteenth anniversary of John's death, Thoreau acknowledged chronic depression, and also expressed a Hamlet-like conflict about suicide:

> *We are all ordinarily in a state of desperation; such is our*
> *life; ofttimes it drives us to suicide. To how many, perhaps*
> *to most, life is barely tolerable, and if it were not for the*
> *fear of death or* dying, *what a multitude would*
> *immediately commit suicide. (9:222)*

Walden Pond and Post-Traumatic Stress Disorder

Ever since the wartime conditions of "combat fatigue" and "shell shock" – forms of post-traumatic stress disorder – were first identified in the twentieth century, one recommended treatment for PTSD has been rest and rehabilitation. Thoreau intuited this, and Walden Pond became a refuge where he restored himself, in part, from his severe, chronic stress disorder.

In the years following the end of his Walden retreat, Thoreau kept up a daily routine of walking many hours in Walden Woods. On the fifteenth anniversary of his brother's death, he wrote in his journal:

> *There is nothing so sanative, so poetic, as a walk in the woods and fields ... Nothing so inspires me and excites such serene and profitable thought ... I come to myself, I once more feel myself grandly related, and that cold and solitude are friends of mine. ... I come to my solitary woodland walk as the homesick go home ... This stillness, solitude, wildness of nature is a kind of thoroughwort, or boneset, to my intellect. This is what I go out to seek ... There at last my nerves are steadied...* (9:208-09) [4]

Since Thoreau described his "Rough-Smooth" dream (Chapter 4) on an anniversary of John's death, and since his description uses contrasting imagery expressive of the two poles (manic and depressive) of bipolar disorder, it would seem that the PTSD and bipolar disorder are interrelated – that one aggravates the other.

Thoreau experienced recurrent hallucinations which are also related to PTSD. As discussed in the following chapter, he located his hallucinated mountain on top of the real cemetery in which John was interred, effectively obliterating the grave. His description of himself on the summit of the imagined mountain is "Smooth," linking the hallucination to his manic states.

3

A Hallucinated Mountain

A Mountain to Ride Instead of a Horse

"I do not invent in the least," Thoreau insisted of the enormous mountain that he hallucinated repeatedly over the years. *"I can see its general outline as plainly now in my mind as that of Wachusett."* This recurrent tactile-visual hallucination was quite vivid: Thoreau claimed that he ascended it physically once or twice. [1]

In an extensive journal entry about this hallucination when he was forty years old, Thoreau related having experienced it *"for the twentieth time at least"* in the fifteen years since John's death, and set about analyzing its latest recurrence. As he sought to interpret its symbols and associations, Thoreau realized for the first time the meaning of certain key elements, although other aspects eluded him. (10:141-44)

An examination of both the hallucination and Thoreau's analysis of it casts light on the value that this familiar vision had for him as a therapeutic tool. *"I keep the mountain to ride instead of a horse,"* he declared. Such *"rides"* or virtual ascents, in an era before psychotropic drugs, enabled Thoreau to elevate his moods, and it appears that, at least in part, Thoreau was able to induce the mountain-visions on his own. [2]

A Halo of Light

Baffled by the recurrent hallucinations, which probably contributed to his self-diagnosis of *"Insanity"* (reported in connection with the Rough-Smooth dream, Chapter 4), Thoreau sought, somewhat unsuccessfully, to discover the antecedents of this latest appearance: *"Whether anything could have reminded me of it in the middle of yesterday ... I doubt."* (10:141)

Thoreau overlooked a compelling visual phenomenon that he had witnessed two days before. While he was contemplating some *"cheerless-looking slate-colored clouds,"* suddenly *"a low-slanted glade of sunlight from one of heaven's west windows"* moved across the landscape, lighting up one part after another *"with an incredibly intense and pure white light."* Though it was only a *"transient ray"* in an overcast sky, its intensity *"was surprising and impressive, like a halo, a glory in which only the just deserved to live."*

Contemplating this *"serene elysian light,"* Thoreau was reminded of unfulfilled aspirations: *"At the eleventh hour, late in the year, we have visions of the life we might have lived ... It was such a light as we behold but dwell not in !"* (10:133)

The "Burying-Hill"

Thoreau wondered whether the realistic location of his imaginary mountain, atop the Concord cemetery where his brother was interred, might be connected with the hallucination. He almost dismissed the idea. *"It chances, now I think of it, that it* [the mountain] *rises in my mind where lies the Burying-Hill ... but that hill and its graves are so concealed and obliterated by the awful mountain that I never thought of them as underlying it."*

But pursuing this association, Thoreau proposed a symbolic link between cemetery and hallucination: *"Might not the graveyards of the just always be hills, ways by which we ascend and overlook the plain?"* (10:143)

The reference to *"graveyards of the just"* calls to mind the halo of intense light that Thoreau witnessed two days before the hallucination, in which *"only the just deserved to live."* (10:133) The graveyards of the just were, so to speak, revealed to Thoreau as the foundation of his mountain by the glade (flash) of heavenly light that he beheld. His feelings about the just and the unjust, John and himself respectively, derive from the romantic triangle that existed among John, Henry, and Ellen Sewall.

A Symbolic Tombstone

Considering Henry's romantic competition with John, his guilty wish to have Ellen Sewall for himself, and John's guilt-provoking death (Chapter 1), Henry must have doubted that he was one of *"the just* [who] *deserved to live."*

In death as in life, John was Henry's ego-ideal: *"I do not wish to see John ever again – I mean him who is dead,"* Henry wrote to Emerson's sister-in-law Lucy Brown, *" – but that other whom only he wished to see, or to be, of whom he was the imperfect representative. For we are not what we are, nor do we treat or esteem each other for such, but for what we are capable of being."* [3]

While alive, John had been regarded as "saintly minded." Concord's Unitarian minister eulogized John as "radiant with the glory of God." [4] This deification of John by many who knew him helps explain why Henry, sauntering on top of the hallucinated mountain, felt he *"trod with awe the face of a god turned up."* (10:144)

The imaginary mountain, which *"ever smoke*[d] *like an altar with its sacrifice,"* may be considered a symbolic tombstone under which lay the sacrificial victim, the deceased brother. After all, it was Henry who wanted John out of the way to have Ellen to himself. The mountain was not only a monument to honor Henry's deceased ego-ideal, but also a heavy weight, to keep John in his grave. But John wouldn't stay dead in Henry's psyche; he was therefore impossible to bury.

"A Promised Land I Have Not Yet Earned"

Ever resourceful, Thoreau transformed the hallucinated mountain into a poem. Although not one of his finest, it casts additional light on the hallucination's latent content.

Forever in my dream and in my morning thought,
Eastward a mount ascends;
But when in the sunbeam its hard outline is sought,
It all dissolves and ends.
*   * * ***

Perhaps I have no shoes fit for the lofty soil
Where my thoughts graze,
No properly spun clues, nor well-strained mid-day oil,
Or must I mend my ways?

It is a promised land which I have not yet earned.
I have not made beginning
With consecrated hand, nor have I ever learned
To lay the underpinning.
         * * *
It is a spiral path within the pilgrim's soul
Leads to this mountain's brow;
Commencing at his hearth he climbs up to this goal
He knows not when nor how. (10:144)

The poem's dominant theme is inadequacy. The poet has *"no shoes fit for the lofty soil"* and *"no properly spun clues, nor well-strained mid-day oil."* Inwardly as well, the poet feels unworthy. He declares the mountain is a *"promised land"* that he has *"not yet earned."*

The poet's sense of unworthiness may be tied to feeling excluded from the glorious halo of light in which *"only the just deserved to live."* Entranced by a mountain of *"superterranean grandeur and sublimity"* which concealed and obliterated John's grave, Henry could distance himself from guilt over fratricidal fantasies come true. The hallucination covered up the evidence below, while at the summit, it allowed him to reunite with the man of his dreams.

"Floating Through Ornamental Grounds"

Hallucinations are generally regarded ominously by Western mental-health professionals, indicative of psychosis. Many presumably normal persons, however, experience a transitional state of drowsiness just prior to, or upon waking from sleep, in which hypnagogic and hypnopompic hallucinations, respectively, can occur. Thoreau experienced both types.*

For example, he reported a hypnagogic illusion induced while canoeing at night up a small stream in Maine. (Joe Polis, his native guide, was doing the paddling.)

> *It was a splendid moonlight night, and I, getting sleepy as it grew late, for I had nothing to do, found it difficult to realize where I was. ... Being in this dreamy state, which the moonlight enhanced, I did not clearly discern the shore, but seemed, most of the time, to be floating through ornamental grounds... I thought I saw an endless succession of porticoes and columns, cornices and facades, verandas and churches.*

Specifying that *"I did not merely fancy this, but in my drowsy state such was the illusion,"* Thoreau concludes: *"Our minds anywhere, when left to themselves, are always thus busily drawing conclusions from false premises."* [5]

The vision of the great mountain, a hypnopompic hallucination, occurred in the early morning hours when, as Thoreau writes,

> *"there is a gradual transition from dreams to waking thoughts, from illusions to actualities ... [U]ntil we have for some time changed our position from prostrate to erect, and commenced or faced some of the duties of the day, we cannot tell what we have dreamed from what we have actually experienced."* (10:141)

Thoreau's hypnopompic hallucinations were not only spiritually uplifting, but elevated his mood, and were recreational:

---

* *Hypnagogic* hallucinations are experienced while falling asleep, *hypnopompic* while gradually awakening.

"My thoughts are purified and sublimed," he wrote about his mountain, *"as if I had been translated* [transported] ... *I keep this mountain to ride instead of a horse."* [6]

Hound, Horse and Dove: That Cryptic Parable

One reason Thoreau kept the mountain to ride instead of a horse was that he had lost his horse. The missing steed is one of a trinity of lost creatures in a cryptic, much-discussed passage of *Walden:*

> *I long ago lost a hound, a bay horse, and a turtle-dove, and am still on their trail. Many are the travelers I have spoken* [to] *concerning them, describing their tracks and what calls they answered to. I have met one or two who heard the hound, and the tramp of the horse, and even seen the dove disappear behind a cloud, and they seemed as anxious to recover them as if they had lost them themselves.* [7]

Many a commentator has ascribed specific referents to the animal symbols in Thoreau's deliberately obscure parable. By now the list of options is lengthy. One interpretation dating from 1926 considers Edmund Sewall (the *"gentle boy"* in Thoreau's poem "Sympathy") the hound, Ellen Sewall the dove, and John Thoreau Jr. the horse. [8]

One more interpretation could be that, since John meant everything to Henry, hound, horse and dove represent important facets of John's personality, lost to Henry in death.

4

The "Rough-Smooth" Dream

*In dreams we see ourselves naked and acting out our real
characters, even more clearly than we see others awake.*
—A Week on the Concord and Merrimack Rivers [1]

Half a century before Freud, Thoreau recognized the self-
revelatory potential of dreams. *"The nearest approach to
discovering what we are is in dreams,"* he noted at age 23 in his
journal, which is teeming with dream notes from all periods of his
life. (1:253)

In childhood, Thoreau recalled, he had experienced a
vivid, recurrent dream that he knew as "Rough and Smooth." Not
until the fifteenth anniversary of his brother's death did he
confront this alternately terrifying and comforting dream in his
journal, concluding with an astonishing revelation – the self-
diagnosis of *"Insanity."*

"All Satisfaction and Dissatisfaction"

The anniversary of John's death in 1857 awoke the
following recollection:

> *I can remember that when I was very young I used to have
> a dream night after night, over and over again, which might
> have been named Rough and Smooth. All existence, all
> satisfaction and dissatisfaction, all event was symbolized in
> this way. Now I seemed to be lying and tossing, perchance,
> on a horrible, a fatal rough surface, which must soon,
> indeed, put an end to my existence, though even in the
> dream I knew it to be the symbol merely of my misery; and*

then again, suddenly, I was lying on a delicious smooth surface, as of a summer sea, as of gossamer or down or softest plush, and life was such a luxury to live. My waking experience always has been and is such an alternate Rough and Smooth. In other words, it is Insanity and Sanity. (9:210-11; Thoreau's emphasis.)

Thoreau's "Rough-Smooth" dream is particularly important since it was recurrent (signifying an unresolved concern) and took place in childhood (indicating longstanding issues). Thoreau's writing of it for the first time at age 40, during an anniversary depression, strongly suggests that the memory of this dream had a deep-rooted association with his brother.

We cannot ask the dreamer for associations to the dream, but we can turn to Thoreau's journal of the previous day for clues to the dream's latent meanings.

"A Coo's Tongue"

On January 6, 1857, Thoreau related an anecdote:

Beatton, the old Scotch storekeeper, used to say of one Deacon (Joe?) Brown, a grandfather of the milkman, who used to dine at his house on Sundays and praise his wife's dinners but yet prevented her being admitted to the church, that his was like a "coo's (cow's) tongue, rough one side and smooth the other." (9:206) [2]

If this is not enough characterization, Deacon Brown was known to Thoreau's friend and walking companion, Ellery Channing, who wrote a description of him in his copy of *Walden*: "a penurious old curmudgeon ... a human rat." [3]

Was there someone Thoreau knew who praised him, but kept him from an inner sanctum, with a Deacon Brown-like duplicity? There was, and he possessed a gifted tongue. Of Emerson, whose smooth eloquence rubbed him the wrong way, Thoreau had earlier confided to his journal (without naming him):

"One of the best men I know often offends me by uttering made words – the very best words, of course, or dinner speeches, most smooth and gracious and fluent repartees…" Instead of such smoothness, Thoreau wished this friend would cease *"repeating himself, shampooing himself! … It produces an appearance of phlegm and stupidity in me the auditor.* (3:141-42) [4]

Ever since Thoreau had returned to Concord from college, he had seen Emerson regularly. Their relationship was possibly complicated by unconscious homoerotic attractions, but above all Emerson was a father-figure whom Thoreau had "loved" for years. Now he sensed Emerson's inauthenticity, and saw duplicity in the man's mannered ways. A month after journalizing about the "Rough-Smooth" dream, the relationship was once more grinding down:

> *And now another friendship is ended. I do not know what has made my friend doubt me, but I know that in love there is no mistake, and that every estrangement is well founded…*

Thoreau was going through a "Rough" time:

> *I am sensible not only of a moral, but even a grand physical pain, such as gods may feel, about my head and breast; a certain ache and fullness.* (9:249)

Two weeks later, Thoreau compared their friendship to a wrecked ship driving before a gale, *"with a crew suffering from hunger and thirst, not knowing what shore, if any, they may reach."* He felt that his *"planks and timbers"* were scattered, and hoped to make *"a sort of raft of Friendship on which, with a few of our treasures, we may float to some firm land."* (9:276-77)

With *"an aching of the breast,"* Thoreau directly addressed the person causing the gale-force winds: *"You cheat me, you keep me at a distance with your manners. I know of no other dishonesty, no other devil. Why this doubleness?…"* (9:277) We are brought back to Deacon Brown's "coo"-like tongue, rough on one side, smooth on the other – which explains why Thoreau recorded this anecdote at all.

Toward an Interpretation of
the "Rough-Smooth" Dream

The association between *"smooth as the axle of the universe"* and the Rough and Smooth dream was made in Thoreau's psyche in the context of an affect-laden emotional field. Beginning on Christmas Day, 1856, Thoreau had been feeling dispirited. By December 29, his emotional state had worsened: *"Staying in the house breeds a sort of insanity always. Every house is in this sense a hospital. A night and a forenoon is as much confinement to the wards as I can stand."* (9:200)

Analysis of Thoreau's nightmare suggests that "Rough" symbolizes the depressive, and "Smooth" the manic, phases of bipolar disorder. "Rough" and "Smooth," in other words, may be considered symbolic of emotional highs and lows. The low moods apparently could be triggered by perceived duplicity, pretentiousness, and other inauthentic behaviors that Thoreau encountered in his fellow man, be it the gracious Emerson or the superficial men whose property boundaries he surveyed.

Given the terrifying intensity of the "Rough-Smooth" nightmare (which he felt could have *"put an end to* [his] *existence"*), and the self-diagnosis of *"Insanity,"* Thoreau was most likely afflicted with bipolar Type I disorder, the more severe of the two variants. Its diagnosis requires the presence of major depression as well as frank (full or extreme) mania. [5]

"The World-Surrounding Hoop! Faery Rings!"

On occasion, the flight of ideas and stream of associations, characteristic of mania, are so extensive that they obscure the meaning of Thoreau's prose. In his ruminating about Concord's Old Carlisle Road, florid mania is evident:

Road – that old Carlisle one – that leaves towns behind;
where you put off worldly thoughts; where you do not carry

a watch, nor remember the proprietor; where the proprietor is the only trespasser, – looking after his apples! – the only one who mistakes his calling there, whose title is not good; where fifty may be a-barberrying and you do not see one. It is an endless succession of glades where the barberries grow thickest, successive yards amid the barberry bushes where you do not see out. There I see Melvin and the robins, and many a nut-brown maid <u>sashé-ing</u> [sic] to the barberry bushes in hoops and crinoline, and none of them see me. The world-surrounding hoop! faery rings! Oh, the jolly cooper's trade it is the best of any! Carried to the furthest isles where civilized man penetrates. This the girdle they've put round the world! Saturn or Satan set the example. Large and small hogsheads, barrels, kegs, worn by the misses that go to that lone schoolhouse in the Pinkham notch. The lonely horse in its pasture is glad to see company, comes forward to be noticed and takes an apple from your hand. Others are called great roads, but this is greater than they all. The road is only laid out, offered to walkers, not accepted by the town and the travelling world. To be represented by a dotted line on charts, or drawn in lime-juice, undiscoverable to the uninitiated, to be held to a warm imagination. No guide-boards indicate it. No odometer would indicate the miles a wagon had run there. Rocks which druids might *have raised – if they could. There I go searching for malic acid of the right quality, with my tests. The process is simple. Place the fruit between your jaws and then endeavor to make your teeth meet. The very earth contains it. The Easterbrooks Country contains malic acid.* (12:348-49; Thoreau's emphasis.) [6]

Some determinants of this bout of mania can be identified; for example, voyeurism is apparent *("I see... many a nut-brown maid... and none of them see me")*. The passage contains other private references as well, so that other determinants could probably be identified if more biographical particulars were available. [7] At all events, Thoreau's private jokes, combined with imagery he borrows from literary sources (the use of Puck's line from *A Midsummer Night's Dream* tends to associate the magical Old Carlisle Road with Shakespeare's world of shape-shifting and delirium), result in spectacular "circle" metaphors in this passage – classic Daedalian imagery, as we shall see in Chapter 8 ("Love of Circular Patterns").

Whatever the precipitants, by the day's end Thoreau's obsessive defenses came into play, and he concluded his journal entry by resuming his role of natural historian, recording meticulous observations about one particular scrub oak: *"I count two hundred and sixty-six acorns on a branch, just two feet long. Many of the cups are freshly empty now, showing a pretty circular pink scar at the bottom, where the acorn adhered."* (12:351) Thoreau's painstaking observations of natural phenomena restored his equanimity, as he knew it would from long experience.

"A Dandelion Down that Never Alights"

Concerning another bout of mania – evidenced in a letter of 1853 – the precipitants are again unclear. Gozzi makes an unsuccessful effort to interpret this production as that of an "atomized, disintegrated, depersonalized ego," which he says reminds him of Dostoevsky's underground man. [8] Thoreau's friend and devoted follower, H. G. O. Blake, may well have been disconcerted upon receiving this letter of philosophic advice couched in a stream of associations and a soaring flight of ideas. Abruptly, Thoreau began by referring to Blake as

> *Another singular kind of spiritual football,– really nameless, handleless, homeless, like myself,– a mere arena for thoughts and feelings; definite enough outwardly, indefinite more than enough inwardly. But I do not know why we should be styled "misters" or "masters": we come so near to being anything or nothing, and seeing that we are mastered, and not wholly sorry to be mastered, by the least phenomenon. It seems to me that we are the mere creatures of thought,– one of the lowest forms of intellectual life, we men,– as the sunfish is of animal life. As yet our thoughts*

have acquired no definiteness nor solidity; they are purely molluscous, not vertebrate; and the height of our existence is to float upward in an ocean where the sun shines,— appearing only like a vast soup or chowder to the eyes of the immortal navigators. It is wonderful that I can be here, and you there, and that we can correspond, and do many other things, when, in fact, there is so little of us, either or both, anywhere. In a few minutes, I expect, this slight film or dash of vapor that I am will be what is called asleep,— resting! forsooth from what? Hard work? and thought? The hard work of the dandelion down, which floats over the meadow all day; the hard work of a pismire that labors to raise a hillock all day, and even by moonlight. Suddenly I can come forward into the utmost apparent distinctness, and speak with a sort of emphasis to you; and the next moment I am so faint an entity, and make so slight an impression, that nobody can find the traces of me. I try to hunt myself up, and find the little of me that is discoverable is falling asleep, and then I assist and tuck it up. It is getting late. How can I starve or feed? Can I be said to sleep? There is not enough of me even for that. If you hear a noise,— 't aint I, 't aint I,— as the dog says with a tin-kettle tied to his tail. I read of something happening to another the other day: how happens it that nothing ever happens to me? A dandelion down that never alights,— settles,— blown off by a boy to see if his mother wanted him,— some divine boy in the upper pastures.

Well, if there really is another such meteor sojourning in these spaces, I would like to ask you if you know whose estate this is that we are on? For my part I enjoy it well enough, what with the wild apples and the scenery; but I shouldn't wonder if the owner set his dog on me next. I could remember something not much to the purpose, probably; but if I stick to what I do know, then— [9]

"Something to Live for"

A third possible example of a manic attack occurred in 1859, on the occasion of John Brown's raid on Harper's Ferry. Thoreau, a loyal supporter of the abolitionist guerrilla fighter, hypergraphically poured 10,000 words concerning Brown, the antislavery struggle, and the evil of slaveholding into his journal in three days and nights (October 19 to 22, 1859). He said he kept a pencil under his pillow: when he couldn't sleep (another symptom of mania), he would write in the dark.

Mania may be considered, at times, a defense against the weight of underlying depression. The relationship between the two affects is apparent when, in the course of his indignant outpourings, Thoreau wrote of John Brown (whose example he considered inspiring): *"How many a man who was lately contemplating suicide has now something to live for!"* (12:439)

5

Seasonal Affective Disorder: "November Eat-Heart"

Thoreau's earliest essay was a school exercise titled *"The Seasons,"* written at the age of ten. The recurrence of New England's particularly varied seasonal phenomena were of lifelong interest to Thoreau, who evolved from being an observer of the natural cycle to feeling it ever deeper within himself. [1]

In 1841, four years before relocating to Walden, he wrote in his journal:

> *I want to go soon and live away by the pond, where I shall hear only the wind whispering among the reeds It will be success if I shall have left myself behind. But my friends ask what I will do when I get there. Will it not be employment enough to watch the progress of the seasons?* (1:299)

Walden, deliberately structured upon the progression of one year's seasons, begins in summer and ends in spring, *"in which the winter of man's discontent was thawing as well as the earth."* [2]

"The seasons and all their changes are in me," he declared, even as he accumulated masses of objective nature data in his journal. *"After a while I learn what my moods and seasons are."* (10:127)

The following journal entries, excerpted across several autumns in the 1850s, provide evidence of the enormous impact that a seasonal change, the advent of winter, effected in Thoreau's psyche. His chronic November depressions are congruent with the mood disturbance now diagnosed as seasonal affective disorder (SAD).

❧

NOVEMBER 12, 1851: The afternoon was cold and dark, the sun hidden behind clouds, the trees leafless; such a day, Thoreau wrote, *"will almost oblige a man to eat his own heart."* It was a day, he wrote, in which one was obliged to *"hold on to life by your teeth,"* for it was hardly possible to *"ruck up any skin on Nature's bones."* It was the time of year to cut timber for yokes and ox-bows: *"yokes for your own neck. Finding yourself yoked to Matter and to Time."* Each thought became *"a vulture to gnaw your vitals."* He felt *"dry as a farrow cow."* (3:110-11)

❧

NOVEMBER 1, 1852: *"In November, a man will eat his heart, if in any month."* (4:405)

❧

NOVEMBER 27, 1853: Again Thoreau declared, *"Now a man will eat his heart, if ever, now while the earth is bare, barren, and cheerless, and we have the coldness of winter without the variety of ice and snow..."* (5:520-21)

❧

NOVEMBER 25, 1857: *"The cattle in the field have a cold, shrunken, shaggy look, their hair standing out every way, as with electricity, like the cat's."* The deserted pastures, he writes, are bare and frozen. Once again Thoreau invokes the eat-heart month. *"This is November of the hardest kind ... November Eat-heart, – is that the name of it?"* (10:202-03)

❧

NOVEMBER 8, 1858: Upon bare fields *where "not a green leaf was to be seen,"* Thoreau wrote, *"the cattle, lately turned out, roamed restless and unsatisfied with their feed."* Clambering over *"curly-pated"* rocks, Thoreau thought: *"They are all gone surely, and left me alone. Not even a man Friday remains."* What nutriment, Thoreau wondered, could he extract from such slim pickings? *"Starvation stares me in the face."* (11:298)

❧

NOVEMBER 14, 1858: On a bitter day, Thoreau walked to the pond in an icy wind that *"makes the oak leaves rustle dryly enough to set your heart on edge."* A city-dweller placed in this desolate realm, he wrote, *"will know of no fire to warm his wits by. He has no pleasing pursuit to follow through these difficulties, no traps to inspect, no chopping to do."* (11:320)

Seasonal Affective Disorder

Seasonal affective disorder may best be considered multifactorial, in that a number of genetic, psychodynamic, geophysical, and sociocultural phenomena enter into play.

Among the specific variables affecting Thoreau in every eat-heart season were the absence of human contact, the month of November as prodromal to John's winter death, sensory deprivation, and decreased daylight hours.

Numerous studies have demonstrated seasonal peaks in the onset of affective episodes in certain people. The predominant seasons are spring and fall, although other patterns, like Thoreau's, may occur with some consistency over the years.

"I Revive with Nature"

With the sights, sounds and fragrances of spring and summer, it is as if Thoreau came out of hibernation. The importance of the abundant sensory stimuli to Thoreau's affective state is apparent in this late-summer entry of August 17, 1851:

> *My heart leaps into my mouth at the sound of the wind in the woods. I, whose life was but yesterday so desultory and shallow, suddenly recover my spirits, my spirituality, through my hearing. ... I can smell the ripening apples; ... the* Trichostema dichotomum, *– not only its bright blue flower above the sand, but its strong wormwood scent – feed my spirit, endear the earth to me, make me value myself and rejoice...* (2:391-92)

With spring's return, Thoreau felt reborn. *"I revive with nature,"* he wrote; *"her victory is mine."* (8:244) With the Pond's ice cover melting, Thoreau could write: *"Walden was dead and is alive again."* [3]

Thoreau noted, significantly, *"We really have four seasons, each incredible to the other."* (3:233) He sought ways to make the seasons of his life more credible to one another, in order that his moods would disrupt him less. In Chapter 14, we will see how Thoreau's Kalendar project was an attempt to predict and control his seasonal depressions and bipolar mood swings.

6

Mind and Brain

A Winter Afternoon Walk

On a cold January afternoon, the fifteenth anniversary of his brother's death, Thoreau walked from town to Walden Pond just as he often did. En route, as we shall see, he encountered an imaginary companion with whom he walked, and experienced a profound sense of universal harmony. Soon afterward he recalled the recurrent tactile nightmares of his childhood (the "Rough-Smooth" dream of the preceding chapter). Then he accurately diagnosed his mental status and prescribed a rational treatment for his condition.

Psychologically and neurologically speaking, we cannot often make an easy transition from considering the mind to considering the brain, even though we know that mind and brain are one entity viewed from different perspectives. Fortunately, Thoreau was alert to his mental processes – watching them, he said, as intently as a cat watches a mouse – and the record he left of his winter-afternoon walk, discussed at the end of this chapter, particularly illuminates the interrelations of neuron and psyche.

Geschwind Syndrome

Neurological researchers Norman Geschwind and Stephen Waxman, in 1974, summarized and expanded a group of personality traits displayed by temporal-lobe epileptics between seizures. [1] Geschwind syndrome, as it is now called, has also been noted in some persons who are not epileptic but apparently have temporal lobe dysfunction, such as that associated with some forms of bipolar disorder. In a recent, highly apposite study of creative writing and writing disorders, *The Midnight Disease*, to which this chapter is indebted, neurologist Alice W. Flaherty summarizes the traits characteristic of Geschwind syndrome:

> **1.   Hypergraphia,** defined by Flaherty as the overpowering urge to write.[2] Such writing is typically cosmic or philosophical in content.
>
> **2.   A deepened emotional life,** sometimes described as hyper-religious or hyper-philosophical; a sober and humorless hyper-morality.
>
> **3.   Emotional volatility,** including intermittent outbursts of aggression.
>
> **4.   Altered sexual activity** (usually reduced).
>
> **5.   Over-inclusiveness:** excessive attention to detail; the inability to omit anything from an account; emotional viscosity.

It is true that we never picture Thoreau as, for example, talkative or aggressive, and rarely as religious. He did, after all, expend lifelong psychic energy suppressing, concealing or controlling some of these traits. Yet from all indications, I submit that Thoreau's personality included most Geschwind characteristics, if not all.

1.   Hypergraphia. Thoreau was a prolific, voluminous writer. His extensive diaries contain over two million words. Unlike many with hypergraphia, Thoreau's written production was consistently of literary quality. The critic Alfred Kazin quite pointedly quipped, "It is not natural for a man to write this well every day."[3] When hypergraphic, Thoreau's handwriting became increasingly illegible.

2.   Hyper-religiosity. Above and beyond even his involvement in transcendentalism and his absorption in Asian belief systems, Thoreau led a spiritual life on a very high plain. In his recent study, *Thoreau's Ecstatic Witness*, Alan Hodder presents Thoreauvian philosophy as a unique, one-man "ecstatic religion of nature." [4]

An uncompromising idealist, Thoreau was hyper-moral, holding himself and others to unrealistically pure standards. Chastity was such an overridingly important virtue to him that he high-mindedly recommended it to H. G. O. Blake on the occasion of the latter's marriage in 1852. [5]

3. Emotional volatility. Like many depressives, Thoreau appears to have mastered, early in life, the technique of suppressing his rages instantly – directing them inward. As a result, contemporaries seldom if ever observed angry outbursts or impulsive actions in him.

Instead, Thoreau usually reduced his temper by channeling anger into his hypergraphic projects. Raymond Gozzi's observation is accurate: "The main vehicle of Thoreau's aggression was words." The complicated anger he felt at Concord's negative reaction to his choice of jail-time over tax-payment in 1846 eventually found oblique expression in real life, but far more importantly, it fueled "Civil Disobedience" and Thoreau's subsequent abolitionist essays. He delivered his antislavery speeches not in the artless style of a lyceum lecture but "as if it burned him." When Thoreau interrupted his botanical journalizing on June 9, 1854 (and again on the 16th and 17th) to discharge the first draft of *"Slavery in Massachusetts"* almost in one stroke, the pressure of emotion is visible in the altered handwriting. [6]

4. Altered sexuality. Thoreau evidently had no sexual encounters at all during his life. He may at first have been bi-erotically inclined, judging from his reactions to Edmund and Ellen Sewall in 1839-40. If so, his sexual polarity decidedly moved to homoerotic following the death of his brother in 1842.

On the other hand, bi-eroticism may not have been present, for there may not have been any heterosexual pole to speak of. A semblance of heterosexual inclination may have been the product of societal conditioning. As Harding notes in his detailed study of Thoreau's erotic makeup, "Thoreau's heterosexual drive was very low, indeed almost non-existent. His few actions and comments in that direction seem more to have been inspired by a desire to conform to what was expected of a male in his society than by a sexual urge." [7]

5. Over-inclusiveness. Thoreau's urge to include as much data as possible in his Kalendar (Chapter 14) is a striking example of over-inclusiveness in a writing project. (See the illustration.) Even the succinct prose of *Walden* is amazingly inclusive by virtue of its relentless word-play, humor, and multifaceted allusions. Once the reader begins "unpacking" the text, Thoreau's chronicle contains labyrinthine layers of reference.

An Invisible Companion

Thoreau was subject to altered states of consciousness, of the type sometimes observed during temporal lobe seizures of epileptics, in which there is the illusion of the presence of another being or another self. (The usual literary example is the *doppelgänger* that Dostoevsky described in *"The Double."* [8]) Thoreau expressed this phenomenon on one anniversary of his brother's death.

On the afternoon of January 7, 1857, Thoreau walked from his home in Concord to Walden Pond, the same route he had walked virtually every day for years. It was the fifth straight day of windy winter weather and the air was bitterly cold. The pond was a snow field; there were not even any footprints of ice-fishermen on it because it was too cold for them. *"All animate things,"* Thoreau observed, *"are reduced to their lowest terms."* (9:207)

Upon arriving at his pond, it was as if he had come to an open window: *"I see out and around myself."* Thoreau was not satisfied with ordinary windows: *"I must have a true skylight,"* he wrote. *"My true sky light is on the outside of the village."* (9:209; Thoreau's emphasis.)

For Thoreau, there was *"nothing so sanative ... as a walk in the woods."* In the streets of town, almost invariably, he felt *"cheap and dissipated.... But alone in distant woods or fields,"* he felt *"grandly related."*

Thoreau wrote, *"I come to my solitary woodland walk as the homeless go home."* (9:208) Now that he was in his true home on this anniversary of his brother's death, Henry rather naturally encountered the presence of the great comforter with whom he (still) shared the meadows, fields, and woods: *"It is as if I always met in those places some grand, serene, immortal, infinitely encouraging, though invisible, companion, and walked with him."* (9:209)

The phenomena that preceded this imaginary appearance – sensory deprivation, monotony, and overload – were not coincidental. Sensory deprivation is apparent in Thoreau's description of a stillness of nature in which all living beings are *"reduced"* to a vital minimum. Sensory monotony is evident when he reaches the pond and sees it as a trackless snow field. A final antecedent, by the time Thoreau is surrounded by his *"true skylight,"* is sensory overload. It is as if Thoreau has passed through an open window to be engulfed in the environment, leaving humanity behind. *"Our skylights are thus far away from the ordinary resorts of men."* (9:209) In our time, sensory deprivation, monotony, and overload are used experimentally to induce psychosis. Thoreau used them too, not to become psychotic, but to alter consciousness: *"Nothing so inspires and excites me…"*

From a neurological point of view, Thoreau undoubtedly experienced a high level of activity in the brain's temporal lobes, and this inspired his encounters and walks with his imaginary companion. The high level of neuronal stimulation produced a sense of universal bliss, a state sometimes reported in temporal lobe epilepsy and related conditions: *"There, in that Well Meadow Field … All things go smoothly as the axle of the universe."* * (9:210; Thoreau's emphasis.)

Much as the gustatory stimulus of Marcel Proust's "little madeleine" evoked a remembrance of things past, Thoreau's tactile simile elicited an early childhood memory:

> *I can remember that when I was very young I used to have a dream night after night, over and over again, which might have been named Rough and Smooth.* (9:210)

---

* Well Meadow is the actual name of the field in Walden Woods where this experience occurred. There are no coincidences in Thoreau's verbal universe.

Thoreau's neuronal activity undoubtedly stimulated the hippocampus, that part of the temporal lobes vital to memory storage. The stimulation then brought this crucial recollection, stored for more than three decades, so vividly to mind that it became necessary to write it out:

> *All existence, all satisfaction and dissatisfaction, all event was symbolized in this way. Now I seemed to be lying and tossing, perchance, on a horrible, a fatal rough surface, which must soon, indeed, put an end to my existence...* (9:210)

The mortal fear associated with the "Rough" nightmares suggests that the amygdala, the structure in the temporal lobe involved with the emotions, was also stimulated.

Bipolar Disorder vs. Epilepsy

Bipolar (manic-depressive) disorder is a psychiatric condition that produces mood swings, whereas temporal lobe epilepsy is a neurological disorder producing short-lived seizures. Nevertheless, as Flaherty points out, the symptoms overlap to such an extent that it is sometimes difficult to distinguish one condition from the other in order to make a definitive diagnosis. *

The pressured speech that is characteristic of mania, for example, appears to be an oral form of hypergraphia. Emotional volatility with aggressive outbursts is common to both disorders. So are altered sexual behaviors. As evidence of the neurological overlap, Flaherty notes that most of the same anti-convulsant medications routinely used today to help control epileptic seizures have proved helpful in stabilizing the mood swings of bipolar disorder as well. [10]

---

* "Poe and Byron, for instance, have been diagnosed both ways, as biographers try to explain their mercurial temperaments and prolific writing." (Flaherty, 29-30.)

It can be assumed that Thoreau had bipolar disorder rather than temporal lobe epilepsy, since he makes no mention of post-ictal amnesia, which typically accompanies the latter. Nevertheless, his responsiveness to acoustic stimuli, his imaginary companion, and the presence of most Geschwind traits indicate that Thoreau was subject to increased temporal lobe activity.

Self-Diagnosis and Prescription for Treatment

In reporting his "Rough-Smooth" nightmare, as we have noted, Thoreau makes a startling revelation: *"My waking experience always has been and is such an alternate Rough and Smooth. In other words, it is Insanity and Sanity."*

Having provided this excellent, albeit generalized, diagnosis, Thoreau envisions a fit therapeutic regime to treat it: *"Might I aspire to praise the moderate nymph Nature ! I must be like her, moderate."* (9:211)

For years, Thoreau had been swelling his journal pages (over-inclusively) with botanical and seasonal data gathered during long daily walks in the woods and wetlands around Concord. Thoreau's self-therapy would take the form of the Kalendar project discussed later in this book. In order to predict, control and stabilize (or *"moderate"*) his mood swings, Thoreau would undertake the systematic tabulation of the recurrent natural phenomena that he recorded.

7

Mood Imagery: Icarus

The wisdom of some of those Greek fables is remarkable.
... They are the skeletons of still older and more universal
truths than any whose flesh and blood they are for the time
made to wear. ... (1:391-92)

The Life-Myth

For the clinical psychiatrist, accurate diagnosis of an inapparent mood disorder can be a major challenge in cases where it is masked by a longstanding compensatory behavior – by workaholism, substance abuse, or a "stiff upper lip" attitude for example. The psychiatrist then considers a variety of data, searching for clues to a suspected underlying disorder.

Dreams, fantasies, works of art, and literary imaginings may all provide important clues about underlying affective states. In this respect, the psychiatric biographer's procedure is not very different from that of a sensitive literary biographer. As Leon Edel wrote of his craft, the biographer needs to unlock his subject's private mythology by searching for what he calls "the figure under the carpet, the evidence on the reverse side of the tapestry, the life-myth of a given mask." [1]

I submit that the presence of Icarian and Daedalian imagery in Thoreau's imaginative productions provides presumptive evidence of underlying bipolar (manic-depressive) mood swings. This chapter and the next present evidence from his literary imaginings in support of this hypothesis.

A Greek Fable: Icarus and Daedalus

The myth of Daedalus and Icarus, archetypal figures from archaic Greek civilization, may be considered central to Thoreau's life and work – his "covert myth."

Daedalus, an architect and inventor, was exiled from Athens for the attempted murder of his nephew Talos in a jealous rage. With his son, Icarus, he travelled to Crete, where he built for King Minos a labyrinth to contain the monstrous, bull-headed Minotaur.

When Daedalus finally completed the task of building the intricate maze, the tyrant tried to prevent the architect's departure by imprisoning him and his son in a high tower. Daedalus used his ingenuity to escape by constructing wings for both of them, made of feathers and wax.

Despite the father's admonitions to fly neither too high nor too low, Icarus disobeyed and flew toward the sun. The wax melted and he plummeted to his death in the sea. Daedalus escaped to safety and hung up his wings in despair, never to fly again.

The Icarus Complex

Thoreau's classical education made Icarus available as a literary subject. Icarian imagery is used consciously in some poems, for example the beautiful "Smoke," which begins:

Light-winged smoke, Icarian bird,
Melting thy pinions in thy upward flight, ... [2]

The Icarus complex, on the other hand, is found on an unconscious level; Thoreau expresses it creatively by the use of imagery which is Icarian in content, even though it may not allude to the mythic character. For example, Thoreau uses Icarian imagery to conclude a journal passage on the ubiquity of the sky and the value of "elevation": *"...we stand on the summit of our hour as if we had descended on eagle's wings. ... We shall not want a foothold, but wings will sprout from our shoulders, and we shall walk securely, self-sustained."* (1:215)

No doubt significantly, Thoreau as a "self-sustaining" Icarus can do without his father's craft and sprout wings by himself.

But then again, perhaps Icarus does require his father Daedalus. The two are opposite and yet complementary. The next chapter will introduce the idea of a Daedalus complex, complementary to the Icarian; I will suggest that Thoreau embodied both facets in his personality. When they were in balance, Thoreau was euthymic. When the Icarian mode is evident, he was manic or hypomanic. And when Daedalian imagery is foremost, he was depressed.

The Daedalian traits, we shall see, include a mistrust of high-flying Icarian intuition and a need for solid ground; a genius for invention, construction, and design; and fascination with circles and cycles, and with intricate structures such as mazes, labyrinths, spirals, and loops. Thoreau's writings abound in Daedalian as well as Icarian imagery.

The Icarus complex was first described in 1955 by Henry A. Murray, who characterized the Icarian personality as being "multiple, fluent, diffuse, unconventional and extravagant." [3] Murray enumerated characteristic Icarian traits, notably the following seven, all identifiable in Thoreau: [4]

1. **Ascensionism:** a love of flying, floating, heights, birds, and mountains.
2. **Ascension-descension,** a sequence "reminiscent of the great cycles of nature" (Murray).
3. **Cynosural narcissism: a** craving for attention and admiration.
4. **Fascination with fire:** solar and fire imagery and, in some cases, "an abundance of water imagery."
5. **Desire for immortality:** "some form of reascension."
6. **"Original, surprising, child-like, far-fetched, expansive, exaggerated or bizarre" imaginings.**

7. Bi-eroticism and misogyny. *

1. Ascenscionism

My desire for knowledge is intermittent; but my desire ... to bear my head through atmospheres and heights unknown to my feet, is perennial and constant. (2:150-51)

Ascenscionism, according to Murray, refers to the admiration of, and identification with, tall, elevated, or rising entities (such as mountains, trees, sun and stars, birds, or people to be looked up to). *Corporeal* ascenscionism is the extravagant propensity to overcome gravity – to stand on tiptoe, leap, fly, or float in the air.

Thoreau was abundantly endowed with ascenscionism, spiritually and bodily. As a contemporary recalled,

> Once, after a day so stormy that he had not taken his customary outdoor exercise, Henry came flying down from his study when the evening was half spent. He face was unusually animated; he sang with zest, but evidently needed an unrestricted outlet for his pent-up vitality, and soon began to dance, all by himself, spinning airily round, displaying remarkable litheness and agility; growing more and more inspired, he finally sprang over the center-table, alighting like a feather on the other side – then, not in the least out of breath, continued his waltz until his enthusiasm abated. [5]

As we have already seen, Thoreau enjoyed the experience of floating – whether in a boat or a dream – and frequently alluded

---

* Or, in Murray's original terminology, "bisexuality" and "depreciation and enthrallment of women." The latter trait includes seeing women "as objects to be utilized for narcis[sis]tic gains" (Murray, 639).

to it in his writing. In his journal he used this metaphor to convey the transcendental relationship between the material and spiritual realms:

> *This stream of events which we consent to call actual, and that other mightier stream which alone carries us with it, —what makes the difference? On the one our bodies float, and we have sympathy with it through them; on the other, our spirits.* (2:43)

Thoreau felt powerful affinities with trees, mountains, and especially birds. Richard Cook, sorting out Thoreau's similes and metaphors in a quantitative study, discovered that "there are more images in *Walden* that involve birds than of any other single phenomenon – including weather – in the whole of Thoreau's nature imagery." [6] Among many birds, Thoreau compared himself to Chanticleer the rooster, who in the morning *"takes his perch upon the highest rail and wakes the country with his clarion."* (5:216)[7] This image of the crowing cock exemplifies the connection between ascensionism and another Icarian trait discussed in this chapter, cynosural narcissism or the craving for admiration.

Thoreau, who could sense *"the seasons and all their changes"* within him, felt an identity with birds in flight, particularly those in migration. At 23, musing on the end of winter and the soul's final journey, he writes of (but will not "yield" to) a bodily impulse to take off:

> *To-day I feel the migratory instinct strong in me, and all my members and humors anticipate the breaking up of winter. If I yielded to this impulse, it would surely guide me to summer haunts. This indefinite restlessness and fluttering on the perch do, no doubt, prophesy the final migration of souls out of nature to a serene summer, ... winging their way at evening and seeking a resting-place with loud cackling and uproar!* (1:176)

For forty days in 1841, following his brother's death, Henry made no journal entries. This was extremely unusual in an author accustomed to journalize almost daily.

When he broke his silence on February 19, 1842, he used significant horizontal and vertical imagery: *"My path hitherto has been like a road through a diversified country, now climbing high mountains, then descending into the lowest vales. From the summits I saw the heavens; from the vales I looked up to the heights again. ... in adversity I remember my own elevations..."* (1:320) The highs and lows correspond to emotional ups and downs. The next day, pure Icarianism: *"I am like a feather floating in the atmosphere; on every side is depth unfathomable."* (1:321) This depersonalization connects with psychic numbing, a symptom of PTSD, as we have seen. It defended Thoreau against emotional pain. As long as he was in a manic, dissociative state, he could transcend it.

In Chapter 4, we considered the significance of Thoreau's recurrent childhood "Rough-Smooth" dream. In the context of Thoreau's Icarianism, the sensations he described take on full significance. Describing the "Smooth" phase, Thoreau wrote, *"I was lying on a delicious smooth surface, as of a summer sea, as of gossamer or down or softest plush, and life was such a luxury to live."* (9:210-11) Floating suspended on the delicious smooth surface, a form of Icarian ascensionism linked to mania, provided the detachment or psychic numbing that cushioned Thoreau against rough reality, on this anniversary of John's death.

Thoreau similarly described the enormous hallucinated mountain (Chapter 3) in Icarian terms, *"as if it were solidified air and cloud ... [a] rocky, misty summit, secreted in the clouds..."* Solidified air and clouds would have smoothed the ascent to the summit of the mental tombstone that Henry erected for brother John, his ego-ideal. (10:142)

Thoreau longed to look up to a spectacular, heroic Icarian. *"What can be uglier than a country occupied by grovelling, coarse, and low-lived men? No scenery will redeem it."* Any landscape, he declared, *"would be glorious to me, if I were assured that its sky was arched over a single hero."* (3:23-24) That hero, Thoreau imagined several years before Walden Woods, could be the solitary philosopher:

> *Whoever has had one thought quite lonely, and could contentedly digest that in solitude, knowing that none could*

accept it, may rise to the height of humanity, and overlook all living men as from a pinnacle. (1:248)

2. Ascension and Descension

Icarian ascent and descent is particularly evident in his responses to love and death during the erotically charged period from June 1839 to November 1840, the year of Ellen Sewall.

Thoreau's journal entry of June 19, 1840, as remarked earlier, conveys the Icarian bliss of floating on water and gazing skyward – a freedom and clarity of focus that cannot last, he says, because *"mean relations and prejudices"* always enter the picture. (1:144)

The following day, June 20, 1840, Thoreau's emotional rollercoaster is evident.

> *Let us remember not to strive upwards too long, but sometimes drop plumb down the other way, and wallow in meanness. From the deepest pit we may see the stars, if not the sun. Let us have presence of mind enough to sink when we can't swim. At any rate, a carcass had better lie on the bottom than float an offense to all nostrils. It will not be falling, for we shall ride wide of the earth's gravity as a star, and always be drawn upward still ,– semper cadendo nunquam cadit ,– and so, by yielding to universal gravity, at length become fixed stars.* (1:146)

Alternating optimism and pessimism about working things out are reflected in the highs and lows of Thoreau's successive images: *"striving upwards"*; *"drop plumb down"*; seeing the sky *"from the deepest pit"*; *"sink when we can't swim"*; *"lie on the bottom [rather] than float"*; floating, riding and not falling, riding *"wide of the earth's gravity as a star"*; and remaining in suspension *("forever falling, never fallen,"* in the Latin phrase in the passage above – possibly a borrowing from physics).

Thoreau concludes his entry for June 20 by identifying *"two ways to victory,– to strive bravely, or to yield."* Thoreau yielded to John regarding Ellen, and to *"stern respect"* concerning Edmund. The vertical and horizontal imagery used in these journal pages reflects, I would argue, manic-depression regarding the outcome of complex erotic yearnings.

3. Cynosural Narcissism

The term cynosural narcissism, an Icarian trait, was coined from "cynosure," the pole star, the apparent center of the rotating heavens. In this extreme form of narcissism, the individual needs to be spectacular – the one star around whom all the others revolve, the focus of all eyes, the center of attention. In the passage above *("we shall ride wide of the earth's gravity as a star, and always be drawn upward still")*, Thoreau has the fantasy that he will be drawn upward until at length he becomes a fixed star. If he can shine with stellar brightness over the rest of humanity, he needn't be ashamed of his homoerotic attraction to Edmund, nor feel guilty over competing with his late brother for Ellen's affections.

As a creative artist, Thoreau rationalized his cynosural narcissism for posterity in the disingenuous, disarming apology in the opening chapter of *Walden: "I should not talk so much about myself if there were anybody else whom I knew as well."* [9]

4. Fascination with Fire and Sun

Four years before summoning the resolve to move to Walden Pond, Thoreau expressed a longing for a lodge on the southern slope of some hill where, he said, he would gratefully accept all that was his yield between sunrise and sunset. *"In the sunshine and the crowing of cocks I feel an illimitable holiness... The warm sun casts his incessant gift at my feet as I walk along, unfolding his yellow worlds."* (1:202) He wanted a direct relationship with the *"holy light,"* but knew that the journey *"is not a short and easy southern way, but we must go over snow-capped mountains to reach the sun."* (1:250)

Discussing solar imagery in *Walden*, Stanley Edgar Hyman remarks, "the sun is Thoreau's key symbol." The book begins with the theme, *"alert and healthy natures remember that the sun rose clear"* and concludes with the words, *"There is more day to dawn. The sun is but a morning star."* Hyman argues that Thoreau's solar imagery encompasses the two extreme attitudes between which Thoreau evolved – an egocentric view *("I have, as it were, my own sun, and the moon and stars, and a little world all to myself")* and a sociocentric (actually, cosmic) view *("the same sun which ripens my beans illumines at once a system of earths like ours").* [11]

Appeal of Fire. Intending to cook a catch of fish during an outing in late spring when the drought-parched grounds were "as combustible almost as a fire-ship," Thoreau and a friend inadvertently set fire to some 300 acres of valuable Concord woodland. After summoning help, Thoreau watched, losing himself in the *"glorious spectacle"* from a nearby height. Only when nearly surrounded by flames did he descend to join the fire-fighting citizens below. [12]

It seems surprising that Thoreau, an expert outdoorsman, had overlooked the dryness of the dead grass around the pine stump in which he had lit his fire. Yet, assuming Thoreau was momentarily distracted by a guilty memory of his brother's death – he was making the fire in Fair Haven, the brothers' favorite childhood haunt in Walden Woods – it is less puzzling that he could have let the flames get out of hand. [13]

Certainly the medley of Icarian imagery – fire, sunrise, birds, height, water, floating, and flying – in a journal entry that Thoreau penned within a day of mentioning his woods-burning suggests that the accidental fire-setting could have originated unconsciously in a comparable spell of ascensionism. At sunrise, Thoreau imagined soaring over the fog covering Concord as if it were *"nothing but the surface of a lake, a summer sea over which to sail,"* and feeling *"triumphantly"* oblivious to *"the farms and houses of Concord ... at bottom of that sea."* A short while later, bathing in the water and watching a bird in flight, Thoreau watched as the rising sun *"set fire to the edges of the broken cloud ... and they glowed like burning turf."* (2:486-87)

The Walden fire occasioned enormous shame and guilt for Thoreau, who exculpated himself in his journal on an assortment of specious grounds *("I have done no wrong ... and now it is as if the lightning had done it")*. He insisted he had played a role as innocent and even beneficial as nature's: *"When the lightning burns the forest its Director makes no apology to man, and I was but His agent." (2:40) "In the spring I burned over a hundred acres till the earth was sere and black, and by midsummer this space was clad in a fresher and more luxuriant green than the surrounding even. Shall man then despair?" (2:488-89)*

On another journal page, he poeticized the conflagration as a fantasy upon the aurora borealis, imagining his writing as a boon that will benefit (or at least placate) the community: *"Will not my townsmen consider me a benefactor if I conquer some realms from the night, if I can show them there is some beauty awake while they sleep...?"* He depicted the northern lights as a sparkling, wriggling, out-of-control brush fire started by the gods, who bring it under control *"by great exertions."* Whether or not it benefited Thoreau's townsmen, we may view his poetic re-imagining of the event as an act of psychic restoration for himself. After the gods take control, *"the stars come out without fear, in peace." (2:478-79)*

The solar imagery with which Thoreau concludes his thoroughly Icarian essay "Walking" kindles an anticipation of ecstasy, of living for eternity in the present moment: *"So we saunter toward the Holy Land, till one day the sun shall shine more brightly than he has ever done, shall perchance shine into our minds and hearts, and light up our whole lives with a great awakening light, as warm and serene and golden as on a bank-side in autumn."* [14]

❧

Affinity with Water. "An abundance of water imagery" can be characteristic of Icarians.[15] Thoreau's affinity for water is apparent when he writes:

> *There is something more than association at the bottom of the excitement which the roar of a cataract produces. It is allied to the circulation in our veins. We have a waterfall*

which corresponds even to Niagara somewhere within us.
(2:155)

Affinity with water is also apparent in the following:

*I hear the sound of Heywood's Brook falling into Fair
Haven Pond, inexpressibly refreshing to my senses. It seems
to flow through my very bones. I hear it with insatiable
thirst. It allays some sandy heat in me. It affects my
circulations; methinks my arteries have sympathy with it.
What is it I hear but the pure waterfalls within me, in the
circulation of my blood, the streams that fall into my heart?
What mists do I ever see but such as hang over and rise
from my blood? The sound of this gurgling water, running
thus by night as by day, falls on all my dashes, fills all my
buckets, overflows my float-boards, turns all the machinery
of my nature, makes me a flume, a sluice-way, to the
springs of nature... Thus I am washed; thus I drink and
quench my thirst.* (2:300)

Water fascinated Thoreau, and its presence is prominent in
Walden, where the pond – still and centered, yet ever-changing –
serves as the author's alter ego. Thoreau's major works are
structured around going towards, living beside, or departing from
water. Sluggish or rapid, the flow of water is essential to the
brothers' fluvial excursion in *A Week on the Concord and Merrimack
Rivers;* throughout *Cape Cod,* the Atlantic tides' ebb and flow
constantly strew reminders of mortality along the sands.

Daily bathing, for Thoreau, was not simply a pastime, but
"an undescribed luxury." (4:207) After a time immersed in water, he
wrote, *"I begin to inhabit the planet and see how I may be naturalized at
last."* (6:383) He compared his life to a mountain stream which
would await nobody, but which cuts its own channel, and overleaps
all barriers, reaching the sea, with rainbows announcing its victory.

5. Desire for Immortality

"A man," Thoreau declared in his journal, *"should go out [of] nature with the chirp of the cricket or the trill of the veery ringing in his ear. These earthly sounds should only die away for a season, as the strains of a harp rise and swell. Death is that expressive pause in the music of the blast."* (1:302) Elsewhere he considered that *"death ... is a transient phenomenon. Nature presents nothing in a state of death."* (1:327-28)

Thoreau, of course, was human; he rejected the finality of death. Yet his version of immortality does not come with the traditional trappings of the Romantic poet's conceits or the Christian's anticipation of an afterlife beyond this mortal coil. In his philosophy as in his neurosis, Thoreau located the idea of eternity in the perennial cycles of nature, and took comfort in the notion of death as a "transient phenomenon," a perpetual transition.

When Emerson lost his little son to scarlet fever, Thoreau sent a philosophical letter in which he denied death's finality by assimilating it into nature's cyclic processes:

> *How plain that death is only the phenomenon of the individual or class. Nature does not recognize it, she finds her own again under new forms without loss. Yet death is beautiful when seen to be a law, and not an accident – It is as common as life.* [16]

In July 1850 Thoreau generalized about mortality and immortality in his journal:

> *We are ever dying to one world and being born into another, and possibly no man knows whether he is at any time dead in the sense in which he affirms that phenomenon of another, or not.* (2:43)

At times, Thoreau's recurrent depressions could become "stuck" if he lost this faith in the eternal, cyclic exchange of life and death.   This happened in 1853 when a combination of circumstances around the anniversary of his brother's death forced Thoreau to imagine life not as cyclic but as linear, terminable by death in sudden, unthinkable finality.

Thoreau's divergent Icarian and Daedalian images for death are evident when he muses in his journal:

> *Our thoughts are with those among the dead into whose sphere we are rising, or who are now rising into our own. Others we inevitably forget, though they be brothers and sisters. Thus the departed may be nearer to us than when they were present. At death our friends and relations either draw nearer to us and are found out, or depart further from us and are forgotten. Friends are as often brought together as separated by death. (2:130)*

Thoreau's lifelong need to deny the finality of death, the core of his enduring natural philosophy, was surely catalyzed by his traumatic loss of John. He often visualized John's spirit as having passed into the surrounding woodlands, into the mountains.

6. "…Surprising, Childlike, Far-fetched, Expansive…" Imaginings

> *I fear chiefly lest my expression may not be extra - vagant enough, may not wander far enough beyond the normal limits of my daily experience, so as to be adequate to the truth of which I have been convinced.* [17]

Extravagance is possibly the most characteristic element of Thoreau's style. In *Walden* he calls our attention to the root-meaning of the word by inserting a hyphen: extra-vagant, "*wandering beyond.*"

Not bound to conventional ways of acting or speaking, Thoreau's unusual imaginings are often original, surprising, childlike, far-fetched, expansive, or bizarre. To convey unconventional truths, to reveal moral and spiritual verities behind surface appearances, to transport us unexpectedly to some higher frame of reference, Thoreau employed a stylistic strategy of "extravagance," or as Joseph Moldenhauer puts it, "a rhetoric of powerful exaggeration, antithesis, and incongruity." The Thoreauvian style features "hyperbole, wordplay, paradox, mock-heroics, loaded questions, and the ironic manipulation of cliché, proverb and allusion." These devices are "Thoreau's means of waking his neighbors up," Moldenhauer writes. "They exasperate, provoke, tease, and cajole; they are the chanticleer's call to intellectual morning." [18]

Thoreau's unconventional imagination is evident in his fantasies. Justifying the poet's need to keep his spirit open by practicing *"the art of spending a day,"* he declared he should *"shut up my shop and turn* [become] *a watchman,"* as opposed to mundane shopkeeping, *"...if by watching, I can secure one new ray of light, can feel myself elevated for an instant upon Pisgah, the world which was dead prose to me become living and divine, shall I not watch ever?"* (2:471)

The originality of Thoreau's images is startling: *"If I am well, then I see well. The bulletins of health are twirled along my visual rays, like pasteboards on a kite string."* (1:266)

Sunlight and Icarian levitation are coupled in this visual association: *"I am not taken up, like Moses, upon a mountain to learn the law, but lifted up in my seat here, in the warm sunshine and genial light."* (1:158)

As Joseph Wood Krutch observed of paradox, the ability "to unite, without incongruity, things ordinarily thought of as incongruous *is* the phenomenon called Thoreau." [19]

7. Bi-eroticism and Misogyny

Thoreau practiced chastity assiduously. Not the slightest trace of any sexual activity, of any encounters at all, has ever been discovered. Although he loved and needed his mother and two sisters, and although he courted Ellen Sewall in his young manhood, he never ascribed full humanity to any other female. As observed in the preceding chapter, it is possible that Thoreau's initial orientation may have been bi-erotic, considering the stimulation that Edmund and Ellen Sewall successively engendered in him, only a few weeks apart. Supposing this to be the case, then the altered sexuality that characterizes the Geschwind syndrome took the form of a shift to homoeroticism (still without physical outlet) following the death of Henry's brother in 1842, which, as we have seen, aggravated Henry's shame over the failure of his marriage proposal to Ellen, and his guilt over competing with him for Ellen's hand.

Notwithstanding Thoreau's own defensive confusions, there has been no question as to his homoerotic orientation since Harding's definitive essay "Thoreau's Sexuality," which assembled virtually all possible clues in Thoreau's writings (for example, the journal entry cited in Chapter 12, "Enigmatic").

↎

The misogyny that pervades Thoreau's writings is deep-seated and extraordinarily defensive. Harding has amply documented Thoreau's expressed horror of females. From the journal he culled this sampler:

> He thought women lacked "brains" (3:258) and "scruples" (2:116), were "presumptuous" (PJ 1:247), "feeble" (12:356), "trifling" (13:52), and "an army of non-producers" (12:342)...

Harding found only one description of an attractive woman in all Thoreau's writings. Only those women unavailable to him – elderly or married – interested him. [21]

One elder lady whose company pleased Thoreau was Mary Moody Emerson of Concord, more than twice his age, *"[t]he wittiest and most vivacious woman that I know."* (3:113) Ralph Waldo's unmarried, intellectual, outspoken aunt appealed to Thoreau precisely because she distanced herself from the run of socially conditioned women and mocked the stereotypical dumbing-down that was always Thoreau's *bête noire*:

In short, she is a genius, as woman seldom is, reminding you less often of her sex than any woman whom I know. In that sense she is capable of a masculine appreciation of poetry and philosophy. ... Miss Emerson expressed to-night a singular want of respect for her own sex, saying that they were frivolous almost without exception, that woman was the weaker vessel, etc. ... (3:114)

Thoreau imagined physical intercourse (and women's bodies) as unclean and repugnant, and was repelled by the prosaic aspect of ordinary conjugal life:

To be married at least should be the one poetical act of a man's life. If you fail in this respect, in what respect will you succeed? The marriage which the mass of men comprehend is but little better than the marriage of the beasts. (5:369)

This constant deprecation of marriage ("Once while walking across a field... he kicked a skunk-cabbage with his boot and said, *'There, marriage is like that'''*[22]) strongly suggests that a shame- and guilt-provoking experience such as Ellen's rejection only catalyzed a deeply rooted insecurity in Thoreau that must have originated in the family dynamic in which he grew up. He was not being ironic when he observed in his journal, *"I am sure that the design of my maker when he has brought me nearest to woman was not the propagation, but rather the maturation, of the species."* (2:185) [23]

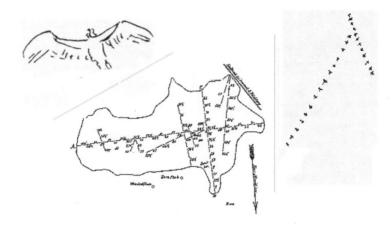

THOREAU'S ICARIAN IMAGERY, I

By permission: Morgan Library (journal sketches). Not to scale.

Left: Fish Hawk, Apr. 28, 1858. Bird imagery abounds in Thoreau's works.

Center: The measure of water: "Walden Pond. A Reduced Plan. 1846." Survey diagram by Thoreau, printed in *Walden* (1854).

Right: Flock of Geese, Nov. 23, 1853. *"...the usual harrow formation..."* (5:518)

THOREAU'S ICARIAN IMAGERY, II
By permission: Morgan Library (journal sketches). Not to scale.
Above: Hill and Moon, May 3, 1852. *"The moon is full. The air is filled with a certain luminous, liquid, white light. ...[The sky] has depth, and not merely distance."* (4:12)

Below: Rainbow over Sun, Feb. 2, 1860. *"Is this what is called a parhelion?"* (13:122)

THOREAU'S DAEDALIAN IMAGERY, I

Journal sketches by permission of the Morgan Library.
Left:
Worm-Bored Limb, Feb. 28, 1855 (7:218)
Air Bubble on an Ice Cake, Feb. 14, 1859 (11:447)
Lichen on Rock "of a peculiarly concentric growth," Aug. 9, 1860 (14:27)

Right:
Pitch Pine Cone Base, Mar. 27, 1853 (5:58)
Pine Cone Base, Jan. 25, 1855 (7:144)

Daedalian Imagery, II

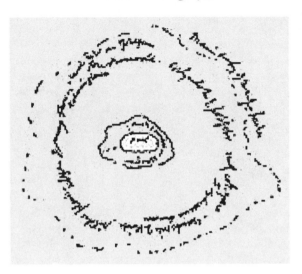

This Daedalian image in Thoreau's field notes is associated with an underlying depression discussed on page 73.

Possibly feeling the "pressure to fill every available space" that characterizes hypergraphia, Daedalian Thoreau contrived to mimic the topography with his handwriting by jotting part of the legend in a circle, to fit within the border of the area described.

From the center outward, Thoreau's four-part legend reads:

pool

rushes & seed vessels on sphagnum

Andromeda calyculata & poliforia – rust cot[ton] grass – cranberries   2 kinds – pitcher plants – sedges – young spruce – larch \/– all on sphagnum   kalmia glauca

Main body of swamp-bushes

ε

Journal, Aug. 23, 1854 (6:467)
Diagram of Gowing's Swamp, Concord
By permission: Morgan Library.

8

Mood Imagery: Daedalus

Not only is he [man] *curiously and wonderfully wrought, but with Daedalian intricacy. He is lost in himself as a labyrinth and has no clue to get out by...* (1:230) [1]

The Daedalus complex refers to a cluster of interrelated personality traits which are complementary to those found in the Icarus complex. The soaring Icarian's descent from "heavenly" mania may be either gradual or abrupt; he plummets, gets bogged down in a maze of trivia, and undergoes the Daedalian changes described by Thoreau: "Though you may have sauntered near to heaven's gate, when at length you return toward the village you give up the enterprise a little, and you begin to fall into the old ruts of thought, like a regular roadster." (12:347)[2] The Daedalian's interrelated personality traits can include some or all of the following:

1. **An obsessive-compulsive penchant for order:** neatness, exactitude, punctuality, or predictability; a need to keep feelings of murderous rage under control.

2. **An attraction to wetlands**, caves and tunnels, subterranean life and crawling creatures: bogs, swamps, mud, bowels, excrement, reptiles, worms.

3. **A desire for terra firma, a solid grounding**: mistrust of high-flying Icarian intuition; ambivalence about the need to return to familiar routine after risk or adventure.

4. **A genius for invention, construction and design:** the architect, engineer, craftsperson, artist.

5. A love of circular patterns: circles, cycles, spheres, spirals, loops, orbits, returns.

6. Fascination with intricate, circular, and downward- or inward-leading structures: mazes, labyrinths, old pathways, spirals, caves, tunnels.

Thoreau presents compelling evidence of Daedalian traits in all these categories:

1. Obsessive-Compulsive Traits

Unlike the high-flying, spontaneous, impulsive Icarian, the Daedalian tends to be an obsessive-compulsive personality type — "scrupulous, neat, pedantic, meticulous, formal, punctual, and in ethical matters strict to the point of asceticism." [2]

Thoreau's two-million-word, fourteen-volume journal, with its punctual entries,* meticulous measurements, scrupulous integrity, and ascetic morality, attests to his obsessional traits.

Controlling rage. Obsessional traits can be a mechanism for coping with overwhelming anger. Like Daedalus, who pushed his nephew Talos from a high place when outraged, Daedalians may unleash homicidal rage when provoked: *"My thoughts are murder to the State and involuntarily go plotting against her,"* Thoreau told a

---

* When Thoreau became ill or depressed, his usual daily entries were sometimes diminished to a sentence or two, or else there were long gaps. For example, following his brother's death, he made no entries for more than a month (Jan. 9 –Feb. 19, 1842). Another example is July 1854, when Thoreau was ill with an undiagnosed (tuberculosis-related?) malady which left his usually sturdy legs weak and limited his daily walks. As Emerson accurately observed, "The length of his walk uniformly made the length of his writing. If shut up in the house he did not write at all" ("Thoreau," 431). Conversely, when Thoreau was hypomanic or manic, his writings could become hypergraphic and over-inclusive, for example on April 10, 1853 (letter to H. G. O. Blake) and Sept. 24, 1859 (12:348-49); see Chapter 4.

crowd in his ringing denunciation of the fugitive slave law, "Slavery in Massachusetts." And in his "Plea for Captain John Brown," Thoreau asserted to a large audience, *"I do not wish to kill nor to be killed, but I can foresee circumstances in which both these things would be by me unavoidable."* [3]

Scatological fascination. Thoreau manifested the compulsive's anal-erotic fascination with excrement: *"What have we to boast of? We are made the very sewers, the cloacae, of nature."* (2:9) Elsewhere he wrote, *"the filth about our houses ... is quite offensive often when the air is heavy at night. The roses in the front yard do not atone for the sink and pigsty and cow-yard and jakes in the rear."* (4:133)

He described the "deep cut" dug for the Fitchburg Railroad near Walden Pond as *"foecal and stercoral"* and compared the spring thawing of this frozen clay-and-sand bank to a bowel movement – and to the creative process:

> *So the poet's creative moment is when the frost is coming out in the spring, but, as in the case of some too easy poets, if the weather is too warm and rainy or long continued it becomes mere diarrhoea, mud and clay relaxed. The poet must not have something pass his bowels merely; that is women's poetry. He must have something pass his brain and heart and bowels, too ... There is no end to the fine bowels here exhibited,—heaps of liver, lights, and bowels. Have you no bowels? Nature has some bowels.* (3:165) [4]

Thoreau sought to steer clear of the *"slimy benignity"* of a certain social reformer *"with which he sought to cover you before he swallowed you and took you fairly into his bowels. It would have been far worse than the fate of Jonah. I do not wish to get any nearer to a man's bowels than usual. I do not like the men who come so near me with their bowels. ... It is the most disagreeable kind of snare to be caught in. Men's bowels are far more slimy than their brains."* (5:264-65)

2. Attraction to Wetlands

Primordial life fascinates the Daedalian, who is drawn to earthy, mucky, dark places – swamps, bogs, tunnels, caves, and underground passageways.

Daedalian images pertaining to sewers, swamps, and reptiles appear frequently in Thoreau:

> *We are conscious of an animal in us, which awakens in proportion as our higher nature slumbers. It is reptile and sensual, and perhaps cannot be wholly expelled; like the worms which, even in life and health, occupy our bodies. Possibly we may withdraw from it, but never change its nature. I fear that it may enjoy a certain health of its own; that we may be well, yet not pure.* [5]

Thoreau's passion for swamps when he was depressed runs throughout his journal:

> *Would it not be a luxury to stand up to one's chin in some retired swamp for a whole summer's day, scenting the sweet-fern and bilberry blows, and lulled by the minstrelsy of gnats and mosquitoes? ... Why be eagles and thrushes always, and owls and whip-poor-wills never?* (1:141-42)

Thoreau most often found swamps uplifting:

> *Beck Stow's Swamp! What an incredible spot to think of in town or city! When life looks sandy and barren, is reduced to its lowest terms, we have no appetite, and it has no flavor, then let me visit such a swamp as this, deep and impenetrable, where the earth quakes for a rod around you at every step, with its open water where the swallows skim and twitter...* (4:231)

Imagery of Depression. In at least one instance, however, he did not find uplift, and depression remained. On August 23, 1854,

Thoreau took himself *"to examine the middle of Gowing's Swamp"* in the course of his local scientific excursions.

Thoreau sketched Gowing's Swamp as a concentric set of rings.* (See the illustration, p. 68.) It would be hard for a reader of his accompanying journal description to ignore the swamp's sexual symbolism. [6]

The froth-covered pool in the middle (the center circle) was ringed by a thick border of rushes *"on a dense bed of quaking sphagnum, in which I sank eighteen inches in water, upheld by its matted roots, where I fear to break through."* (6:467) Standing precariously, Thoreau observed that his border ring (encircling the pool in the sketch) was in turn surrounded by a 100-foot-wide bog of grasses and cranberry shrubs, also rooted in the sphagnum moss. Beyond this (at the dotted border in Thoreau's sketch), the sphagnum bed supported ferns and blueberry shrubs, the *"bushy and main body of the swamp."* (6:467)

Thoreau was not visiting Gowing's Swamp for spiritual renewal. As a nature observer, he was taking advantage of a protracted drought – when swamps were turning into terra firma – to *"walk where in ordinary times I cannot go."* This notwithstanding, the relationship between Daedalian imagery and an underlying depression is evident in Thoreau's case when we consider the concentric image in the context of two journal entries written a few days before and after his date at Gowing's Swamp. Both passages explicitly describe depression, low self-esteem, worthlessness, and guilt.

On August 18, five days previously, Thoreau expressed inexcusable moral guilt over having killed a box-tortoise (*Cistudo*) for scientific examination.

> *I have just been through the process of killing the cistudo for the sake of science; but I cannot excuse myself for this*

---

* Thoreau's fatal pneumonia was the result of catching cold while counting rings on tree stumps on a glacial December day in 1861 – a Daedalian fascination with concentric patterns.

> *murder, and see that such actions are inconsistent with the*
> *poetic perception, however they may serve science, and will*
> *affect the quality of my observations. I pray that I may*
> *walk more innocently and serenely through nature. No*
> *reasoning whatever reconciles me to this act. It affects my*
> *day injuriously. I have lost some self-respect. I have a*
> *murderer's experience in a degree.* (6:452)

Depression is again apparent in the minimal self-esteem (and doubts about his generativity) recorded in a journal passage five days after the swamp excursion.

> *In my experience, at least* of late years, *all that depresses*
> *a man's spirits is the sense of remissness, – duties neglected,*
> *unfaithfulness, – or shamming, impurity, falsehood,*
> *selfishness, inhumanity, and the like.*
> 　　*From the experience of late years I should say that a*
> *man's seed was the direct tax of his race. It stands for my*
> *sympathy with my race. When the brain chiefly is*
> *nourished, and not the affections* [emotions], *the seed*
> *becomes merely excremental.* (6:483;　Thoreau's
> emphasis.)

Unquestionably, external events all during the summer of 1854 fueled a continuing depression. In June, Thoreau's disgust and rage over his state's compliant rendition of the fugitive slave, Anthony Burns, and the pious hypocrisies used to justify its action, spilled over into journal pages otherwise devoted to botanizing:

> *The sight of that political organization called*
> *Massachusetts is to me morally covered with scoriae and*
> *volcanic cinders, such as Milton imagined. If there is any*
> *hell more unprincipled than our rulers and our people, I feel*
> *curious to visit it. Life itself being worthless, all things with*
> *it, that feed it, are worthless. ... I have found that hollow*
> *which I had relied on for solid. (6:358)*

In addition, Thoreau undoubtedly experienced an author's letdown, aggravated by feelings of insecurity and high anxiety, following the publication on August 7 of his often-delayed masterwork, *Walden*, when he permitted himself only two words in his journal: *"'Walden' published."* His dread that this valuable seed might be spilled on sterile ground (like his first published book, a commercial flop) could lie behind the journal comment, "the seed becomes purely excremental."

Coming on the heels of these agitating concerns, Thoreau's precarious visit to the quaking, scum-covered waterhole in hell's central circle is presumptive evidence of a depression affecting his gonads and bowels. By assuming guilt over killing a swamp reptile, Thoreau perhaps mitigated his impotent rage against a hypocritical government. Additionally, we might speculate that Thoreau thereby mitigated possible guilty feelings over symbolically murdering his father-figure, his sometime mentor Emerson, with the publication of a literary work of independent maturity.

3. Desire for a Solid Grounding

With their predilection for getting bogged down and their trepidation over taking wing, Daedalians have an inordinate need for *terra firma* to feel mentally grounded. Thoreau expressed this early in *Walden:*

> *Let us settle ourselves, and work and wedge our feet downward through the mud and slush of opinion, and prejudice, and tradition, and delusion, and appearance, that alluvion which covers the globe, through Paris and London, through New York and Boston and Concord, through church and state, through poetry and philosophy and religion, till we come to a hard bottom and rocks in place, which we can call reality, and say, This is, and no mistake...* [7] *

---

* This passage reminded F. O. Matthiessen of D. H. Lawrence, who also felt the need for Daedalian grounding at times: "'The promised land, if it

Daedalian Thoreau was able to experience a similar profound satisfaction with a *"rock bottom"* while taking a *"fluvial walk"* immersed in the Assabet River:

> *"Here is a road where no dust was ever known, no intolerable drouth. Now your feet expand on a smooth sandy bottom, now contract timidly on pebbles, now slump in genial fatty mud – greasy, saponaceous – amid the pads."* (4:220)

Mistrust of Icarian freedom. The Daedalian may feel that he can rise to Icarian heights:

> *...the hawk that soars so loftily and circles so steadily and apparently without effort has earned this power by faithfully creeping on the ground as a reptile in a former state of existence. You must creep before you can run; you must run before you can fly.* (3:108)

But the prospect of taking such risks will often check his enthusiasm. In *Walden*, Thoreau recounts trying to inspire a laborer, who made a hard living "bogging" (digging peat) for farmers, to rise above his lot. But he concluded that John Field, whom he depicts in Daedalian imagery, was *"not to rise in this world, he nor his posterity, till their wading webbed bog-trotting feet get* talaria [winged sandals] *to their heels."* Thoreau saw Field as mired in his *"Irish poverty"* and *"boggy ways."* [8]

---

be anywhere, lies away beneath our feet. No more prancing upward. No more uplift.'" Lawrence's discovery, according to Matthiessen, "was quickened by watching and almost identifying himself with the downward thrust into the earth of the feet of Indian dancers" (*American Renaissance* [1941], New York: Oxford Univ. Press, 1968, 165).

4. Invention, Construction and Design

Daedalus sometimes symbolized the "Divine Architect" in medieval Christianity, and Daedalians are fascinated with the design and construction of buildings and other structures, including the structuring of open areas and communities. Thoreau's talent for literary architecture was noted by Channing, his walking companion and first biographer: "The impression of the *Week* and *Walden* is single, as of a living product, a perfectly jointed building, yet no more composite productions could be cited." Like these books, Channing found that Thoreau's essays "Wild Apples" and "Autumnal Tints" possessed "unity of treatment," and were products of Thoreau's "constructive, combining talent." [9]

In the first chapter of *Walden*, Thoreau expressed his view that architectural beauty gradually grows *"from within outward, out of the necessities and character of the indweller, who is the only builder,— out of some unconscious truthfulness, and nobleness, without ever a thought for the appearance... The most interesting dwellings in this country, as the painter knows, are the most unpretending, humble log huts and cottages of the poor commonly..."* [10]

5. Love of Circular Patterns

The Daedalian is intrigued by spirals and circles, and Thoreau's devotion to these symbols has occasioned considerable comment from scholars. As Charles R. Anderson wrote in *The Magic Circle of Walden:*

> Orbs, spheres, circular paths and flights, daily and seasonal cycles, orbiting stars and ripples on water – all these form an important part of Thoreau's subject matter and provide him with another way of looking at the world. The imagery ranges from insects to the cosmos and is applied to a great variety of things: animals, plants, ponds, sights, sounds, people. The very structure of his book

[*Walden*] is circular, almost a Ptolemaic system of cycles and epicycles..." [11]

Anderson cites a journal entry in which Thoreau uses circular imagery to convey his idea of the soul's centrality:

All things, indeed, are subjected to a rotary motion, either gradual and partial or rapid and complete, from the planet and system to the simplest shellfish and pebbles on the beach; as if all beauty resulted from an object turning on its own axis, or others turning about it. It establishes a new centre in the universe. As all curves have reference to their centres or foci, so all beauty of character has reference to the soul, and is a graceful gesture of recognition or waving of the body toward it. (1:332)

The circularity inherent in the walks Thoreau loved to take, as well as in "the history of his life, and even ... in the pattern of his most characteristic prose and the structure of some of his controlling ideas," has been analyzed by John C. Broderick, who observes that *Walden* "might be regarded as a year-long walk, for as in his daily walk Thoreau moved away from the mundane world of the village toward one of heightened awareness and potentiality, only to return spiritually reinvigorated, so *Walden* records an adventuring on life which structurally starts from and returns to the world of quiet desperation." [12]

Thoreau's most effective writing, Broderick notes, follows the "'out-and-back' movement" of the "well-loved walk" or excursion. "*Our voyaging is only great circle-sailing,*" Thoreau wrote in *Walden,* while in "*Walking*" he affected to complain: "*Our expeditions are but tours, and come round again at evening to the old hearth-side from which we set out. Half the walk is but retracing our steps.*" Broderick notes that "a geometric design of the life of Thoreau would run to loops and curlicues. Concord was home base for a series of forays into the larger, more or less alien world." [13]

Closely allied to a preoccupation with circles, spirals and mazes, the Daedalian may also manifest a fascination with the "strange loop," a type of abstract structure identified by the physicist-author Douglas R. Hofstadter. In Hofstadter's definition, this phenomenon occurs "whenever, by moving upwards (or downwards) through the levels of some hierarchical system, we unexpectedly find ourselves back where we started." A strange loop, he specifies, may be created in any complex structured system, "in various media and in varying degrees of richness." [14]

Discussing *Walden*, Sherman Paul points out a hidden springtime at the beginning that may qualify that book's seasonal cycle as a strange loop:

> When he [Thoreau] went to the pond in March, 1845, he had already felt the influence of "the spring of springs", he had overcome his "torpidity"; ... and had again become a "child." Though Thoreau buried this spring in "Economy," and deliberately began his account with summer, with his going to the pond to live on Independence Day, the imagery of the melting pond, the returning birds, and the stray goose were the same as in his second "Spring." This additional season, of course, made it possible for Thoreau to recapitulate the entire history of his life from youth to maturity: the first spring, the dewy, pure auroral season of the Olympian life, was true to his youth, and the subsequent seasons and the second spring were the record of the growth of consciousness and of his conscious endeavor to earn the new world of his springtime again. [15] *

The universe in which Thoreau felt free to construct strange loops and other forms of chutes-and-ladders was, of course, the world of words. Any page of Thoreau's prose is replete with plays on words, *double entendres*, concealed meanings, and

---

* Lines from T.S. Eliot's "Little Gidding" come to mind: We shall not cease from exploration / And the end of our exploring / Will be to arrive where we had started / And know the place for the first time.

etymological short-circuits. Thoreau's puns and aphorisms, as Hyman puts it, "tend to make their point by shifting linguistic levels." [16]

6. Fascination with Mazes and Labyrinths

Like other Daedalians, Thoreau was intrigued by mazes – for example, the one he saw in snow-covered pitch pines: *"It is a still white labyrinth of snowy purity, and you can look far into its recesses under the green and snowy canopy,– a labyrinth of which, perchance, a rabbit may have the clue."* (11:390) He delighted in the wild beauty and solitude of Concord's Estabrook Country, depicting its old, irregular roads and paths as mazes:

> *...for my afternoon walks I have a garden ... mile after mile of embowered walks, such as no nobleman's grounds can boast, with animals running free and wild therein as from the first,– varied with land and water prospect, and, above all, so retired that it is extremely rare that I meet a single wanderer in its mazes.* (2:38)

In early civilizations, the construction and ritual circumambulation of a labyrinth were essential to the creation of a city. According to Jill Purce in *The Mystic Spiral*, this ritual symbolized the original cosmic creation, for "when a space is set aside or delineated it is ordered, carved out from the surrounding chaos, and so sanctified." The labyrinthine spiral-circular movements provided early inhabitants with a means for becoming centered in their wanderings through space and time, by guiding them both from and to their place of origin. In this sense, the maze was a mandala. As Purce observes, "the essence of a labyrinth is not its outward form, its delineating stones and hedges, but the movement it engenders." [17]

Thoreau, moving in his own labyrinthine circumambulations, centered himself by sounding depths, measuring snowdrifts, and dating the tree swallow's migrations. By such minute, painstaking, Daedalian attention to grounding facts, he transformed Concord into *"the most estimable place in all the world,"* (9:160) and created *"Cosmos* [order] *out of Chaos."* Like the first cities' founders in their labyrinthine walks, Thoreau found *"our experience does not wear upon us. It is seen to be fabulous or symbolical, and the future is worth expecting."* Encouraged, he set out, again and again, to climb *"the mountain of the earth,"* saying, *"my steps are symbolical steps, and in all my walking I have not reached the top of the earth yet." (5:35)* [18]

Icarus and Daedalus: Psychodynamics

The hypothesis that Icarian imagery is presumptive evidence of an underlying mania, and Daedalian imagery of depression, is worthwhile and should be tested. Such imagery can be found in the work of many artists.

Icarian imagery, seen in Thoreau's sketches of sun, water, and birds, is prevalent in the floating and flying brides and bridegrooms of Marc Chagall's paintings. A master of mazes, M. C. Escher, drew Daedalian figures who are endlessly ascending and descending, but going nowhere.

Psychodynamically, the absence of woman in the Greek myth is noteworthy. Possibly the modulating feminine presence is absent in males who have bipolar disorder. Perhaps Thoreau had to exclude his intrusive mother from his emotional inner sanctum. [19]

Another psychological observation: Daedalus in the legend is an impulsive, jealous, homicidal man. What son would heed the admonitions of a murderous father, no matter how divine an architect?

9

Tuberculosis and Depression

Any chronic, malignant, degenerative, metabolic or infectious disease can lead to depression. Thoreau's pulmonary tuberculosis is a case in point – if it could be proved that he had the illness.

The diagnosis of consumption, as the condition was called prior to 1839 (when Schönlein first described tubercles in the lungs of those affected) was based on clinical symptoms. These included a chronic productive cough, emaciation (as the earlier name implies), weakness, fatigability, and fever. Thoreau suffered from all these, especially in his final years.

Consumption was the leading cause of death in Concord at that time, and since its contagious nature was not known, those afflicted were not isolated from others; consequently, it ran in families. The Thoreau family was not exempt. Grandfather John Thoreau died from it in 1801, Henry's sister Helen in 1849, and it contributed to the death of John Jr., according to Harding. (Nevertheless, infection by a virulent strain of *Clostridium tetani* is sufficient to explain the swiftness of his death.) [1]

Modern medicine validates the clinical impression with bacteriology (microscopic examination of cultured sputum) and radiology. Bearing in mind that Thoreau's condition was diagnosed before such techniques were available, the term "tuberculosis" is a presumptive diagnosis.

Thoreau's first bout with an illness resembling tuberculosis occurred in May 1836, when a severe case of "bronchitis" caused him to come home from college. He returned to dormitory life at Harvard in September, but was plagued by recurring illness.

In February 1841 bronchitis once again occurred, and Thoreau was confined to home. His health was precarious. When he left Concord for Staten Island for a time in 1843, another bronchitis-type episode led to a month's confinement. Chronic drowsiness made it difficult to read or write as much as usual. *"I must still reckon myself with the innumerable army of invalids,"* he informed Emerson. [2]

A perplexing condition (probably tuberculosis-related) developed in the spring of 1855: a weakness of the legs made it almost impossible for him to continue his daily walks. In June he wrote to Blake:

> *I have been sick and good for nothing but to lie on my back and wait for something to turn up, for two or three months. ...I should feel a little less ashamed if I could give any name to my disorder, but I cannot, and our doctor cannot help me to it, and I will not take the name of any disease in vain. ... I expected in the winter to be deep in the woods of Maine in my canoe long before this, but I am so far from that that I can only take a languid walk in Concord streets.* [3]

Emerson remarked of Thoreau "the length of his walk uniformly made the length of his writing. If shut up in the house he did not write at all." Perhaps the frequency of his journal entries likewise corresponded to the frequency of his walks, which would necessarily have been curtailed by illnesses, among other disruptions.

Harding's biography continues the story of Thoreau's consumption into the summer of 1855:

> When he visited Alcott in Boston on the Fourth of July, Alcott noticed his illness and thought he acted 'shiftless' [unenergetic] for the first time in his life. His daily journal entries diminished often to but a sentence and sometimes disappeared altogether for a week at a time. He lost his ebullient optimism for a time and complained often of his loneliness. He felt weak enough that he gave up surveying almost entirely... [4]

As the winter of 1861 progressed, Thoreau's health further deteriorated after a field trip in frigid weather aggravated a cold he had caught into bronchitis, which settled into pneumonia. Throughout the ordeal, Thoreau maintained an outer composure that his family and friends found remarkable. Thoreau's sister Sophia remarked:

> During his long illness I never heard a murmur escape him ... his perfect contentment was truly wonderful. [5]

In Thoreau's final days, sleeplessness kept him uncomfortable, and he "wished his bed were in the form of a shell so that he might curl up in it." [6] Here if anywhere, Daedalian imagery makes it possible to identify his underlying affect.

৵

Depression and tuberculosis have an adverse effect on each other. Thus, when Thoreau was stressed following John's death in 1842, his pulmonary condition flared up. When his usually sturdy legs weakened in 1855, probably as the result of tuberculosis, he became depressed.

Thoreau's penchant for the out-of-doors ameliorated both disorders, not only on account of the salubrious effects of fresh air and sunshine, but because he was away from the deleterious effects of the fine graphite dust created by the Thoreaus' home-based pencil lead-grinding business, which would aggravate the pulmonary disease and thereby intensify his depression.

"The care of the body is the highest exercise of prudence," wrote Thoreau, who was aware of what is now called psychosomatics. In 1841, after being confined by "bronchitis," he wrote: *"If I have brought this weakness on my lungs, I will consider calmly and disinterestedly how the thing came about, that I may find out the truth and render justice."* (1:221)

10

The "Cuttlefish" Defense

"Our Sin and Shame"

Deliberately obscure at times, Thoreau likened himself to the sea creature which releases an inky self-protective substance: *"I live the life of a cuttlefish; another appears, and the element in which I move is tinged and I am concealed."* (4:315)

The ink that poured from Thoreau's pen dried on the page in a lifelong cascade of words, millions of them. Behind the artful persona which those words formed, few got a good look at the real man. *"The impenetrable shield"* (1:106) worked.

Although Thoreau typically denied it, the persona he constructed left him lonely: *"I pine for one to whom I can speak my first thoughts; thoughts which are no better nor worse than I."* (4:315; Thoreau's emphasis.) Thoreau found human contacts perilous. In passages like the following, a reader may glimpse Thoreau's lonely, supersensitive psyche as experienced in periods when he was not manic, hypomanic, or in a state of denial:

> *What if we feel a yearning to which no breast answers? I walk alone. My heart is full. Feelings impede the current of my thoughts. I knock on the earth for my friend. I expect to meet him at every turn; but no friend appears, and perhaps none is dreaming of me.* (7:416-17)

Thoreau's unusual sensitivity and his consequent vulnerability are succinctly characterized by Richard Bridgman: "His tears when his mother suggested he seek his fortune in the world, his falling ill with sympathetic lockjaw after the death of his brother, John, his long brooding on the character of friendship, his confessional poetry, all attest to the profundity of his feelings. But reserved and proud, he tried to protect himself from the disapproving world." [1]

Behind the persona that Thoreau perpetually constructed hid an awkward, self-doubting man like any man – like "the mass of men" he wrote of. To an admirer who wished to pay him a visit, Thoreau wrote discouragingly: *"You may rely on it that you have the best of me in my books, that I am not worth seeing personally – the stuttering, blundering, clodhopper that I am."* [2]

Ongoing feelings of shame in his life made intimacy with others difficult: *"Our sin and shame prevent our expressing even the innocent thoughts we have."* (4:315)

He could not pinpoint its source, but felt that *"a sense of unworthiness ... possesses me, not without reason."* (2:101)

These feelings of shame, particularly in his young manhood when his identity was far from settled, were often stimulated by factors in Thoreau's personal, family and town life, as we have seen. They can only have been exacerbated by public mockery of his early work as being a shallow imitation of Emerson, as in the literary satire *A Fable for Critics* (1848) by the poet and critic James Russell Lowell:

> There comes [Thoreau], for instance; to see him's
> rare sport,
> Tread in Emerson's tracks with legs painfully short;
> How he jumps, how he strains, and gets red in the face,
> To keep step with the mystagogue's natural pace!
> He follows as close as a stick to a rocket,
> His fingers exploring the prophet's each pocket.
> Fie, for shame brother bard; with good fruit of your own,
> Can't you let Emerson's orchards alone? [3]

This *ad hominem* caricature – part of a very long doggerel that trivialized numerous writers including Cooper and Poe – appeared at the exact time when the 31-year-old Thoreau was striving to sever his dependency on Emerson and be regarded as an original author.

"A Soliciting Wood-God"

When he approached manhood, Thoreau's vocational identity was unclear. Doctor, lawyer, educator or minister were the respectable professions for a Harvard graduate in those days, but none of these suited him (except school-teaching, which he tried briefly). At Walden, he became aware of his vocation as a writer, and of his special task – correlating human nature with nature. This correlation, as will be more fully discussed later, he accomplished primarily via transcendental simile: *"The life in us is like the water in the river. It may rise this year higher than man has ever known it, and flood the parched uplands; even this may be the eventual year, which will drown out all our muskrats."* [4]

One of Thoreau's muskrats was homoeroticism. Before John died, Henry had fallen in love with Edmund Sewall, as we have seen, and composed the poem "Sympathy" in his honor. Next, as we have also seen, Thoreau fell in love with Edmund's sister Ellen, proposed to her after she turned his brother down, and was turned down also. After John's death, women – aside from his family – played scant roles in Thoreau's life and almost entirely negative ones in his writings (Chapter 7, "Misogyny").

It is likely that Thoreau's homoeroticism complicated his relationship with Emerson. Emerson compared his young friend to "a soliciting wood-god who enticed him into vast caves and idle deserts, depriving him of his memory, and left him naked, braiding vines, with twigs in his hand." "Very seductive are the first steps from town to the woods," Emerson wrote, "but the end is want and madness." (JMN 10:344)

Their unresolved homoerotic needs and fears must have frightened and frustrated both. Thoreau found Emerson formal, reserved, distant, at times scornful, *"ridiculously stately."* Emerson found his protégé "stubborn," "implacable," "always manly and wise but rarely sweet," and wrote that the oppositional Henry could be "military." Thoreau "required a little sense of victory, a roll of the drums to call his power into full exercise." (JMN 13:183)

Thoreau may have had both homo- and hetero-erotic feelings, but his abstention from sexual practice appears to have been permanently reinforced after John Jr. died. As Howarth writes:

> This dead brother, who had been his best of friends, virtually another self, was Henry's ideal of youth and chastity; his memory became a substitute for love, marriage, and most other commitments. [5]

11

THE "AS-IF" PERSONALITY

Writing in the early twentieth century, the psychoanalyst Helene Deutsch described a character type "in which the individual's emotional relationship to the outside world and to his own ego appears impoverished or absent." Individuals with this emotional disturbance, she observed, unconsciously imitate the thought, affect and behavior of others as a substitute for their own lack of emotion, for feelings would oblige them to engage in a two-way social interaction. Deutsch called this the "as-if" personality, because "the individual's whole relationship to life has something about it which is lacking in genuineness and yet outwardly runs along 'as if' it were complete." [1]

How can Thoreau, of all people, be "lacking in genuineness"? I do not dispute the view that, if anything, the author of *Walden* and "Civil Disobedience" turned his life into a quest for "genuineness." Nor can it be said that Thoreau's deliberately eccentric life "outwardly ran along as if it were complete." He did not want a conventionally "complete" life. Yet in his psyche, as we have seen, he was vulnerable. He needed others' validation. He ached for emotional reciprocity and was highly sensitive to other people's disdain, real or perceived. He idealized relationships unrealistically; expecting Friendship, he was disappointed in friendships. Thus, although admittedly the label "as-if" might be misleading, there is a mass of evidence linking Thoreau to the key characteristics of this affective disturbance.

Although Thoreau had a number of close associates during his lifetime, he had only two close friends: his older brother John

Thoreau, Jr. until 1842, and his mentor and father-figure Ralph Waldo Emerson beginning in 1837.

His relationship with both was characterized by the imitative mode. Henry mirrored John's way of being in nature throughout his life, even after John died. His mirroring of Emerson, to judge from countless contemporaneous descriptions, was a feat of protective coloration that must have outperformed any cephalopod or chameleon.

Mirroring John

A genial, charming and gregarious man, John was also closely connected to nature. Henry imitated his ways in fields and by the pond, but not with people.

The brothers spent much time together, especially out-of-doors, attended school together, and taught together as young men in the private school they founded.

Over the years, Henry came to identify with John, and adopted his interests in nature – trees, birds, and the progress of the seasons. John taught Henry to recognize birds from their calls and trees by their leaves; where to find Indian arrowheads; and how to be at home, in solitude, beneath the arrowy pines.

The boys' father, described as "a quiet, mousey sort of man," [2] related to his unusual sons with tolerance, but not with enthusiasm. John was not only a devoted older brother, but filled in for their home-bound father, in the field.

Henry's "as-if" personality is apparent not only in the lifestyle he evolved that mirrored John's, but also in his unconscious mimicry of his brother's moribund state in 1842.

This particular mimicry began to express itself when Henry "found himself returning" his brother's "transcendent smile" on the day John died. As we saw in Chapter 1, the smile was not one of bliss, but the "sardonic grin" of death itself, the deadly muscle-contraction of tetanus. As we have also seen, Henry's guilt-aggravated facsimile lockjaw was a psychosomatic conversion disorder originating in his deep identification with, and imitation of, his brother in life.

Henry so idolized his brother that, in a sense, he continued John's life for him after death. Consider the eulogy that was read at John's funeral by Barzillai Frost, minister of the First Parish Church of Concord. As Harding observes, it "could have just as appropriately been read for Henry Thoreau" twenty years later, Henry had assimilated so much of his brother.

> He had a love of nature, even from childhood amounting to enthusiasm. He spent many of his leisure hours in straying over these hills and along the banks of the streams. There is not a hill, nor a tree, nor a bird, nor a flower of marked beauty in all this neighborhood that he was not familiar with, and any new bird or flower he discovered gave him the most unfeigned delight, and he would dwell with it and seem to commune with it for hours. He spent also many a serene and loving evening gazing upon the still moonlight scene and the blazing aurora, or looking into the bright firmament, radiant with the glory of God …
>
> The benevolence of the deceased appeared in his love of animals, in the pleasure he took in making children happy, and in his readiness to give up his time to oblige all. He had a heart to feel and a voice to speak for all classes of suffering humanity; and the cause of the poor inebriate, the slave, the ignorant and depraved, was very dear to him …
>
> Of his religious opinions I must speak with less confidence. He has been affected no doubt by the revolutionary opinions abroad in society in regard to inspiration and religious instructions, as it is very natural the young should. But there has been a tendency of late in his mind, I have thought, to those views which have fortified the minds of the great majority of the wise and good in all ages. (I may be mistaken in supposing that he adopted the

transcendental views to any considerable extent.)
But, however his theories *about* religion were
unsettled, his principles and religious feelings were
always unshaken. The religious sentiment had
been awakened, and he manifested it in his tastes,
feelings and conversation. [3]

Mirroring Emerson

As a young man, Thoreau also imitated Emerson. From
their first meeting in 1837 to the time of Thoreau's death in 1862,
the two men saw each other virtually constantly, even when the
friendship declined after its intense first decade. When Emerson
travelled abroad, he would arrange for Thoreau to live at his house
and look after his family.

This famous mentor, one of America's first intellectual
celebrities, was 15 years older than his protégé, had a charismatic
presence, a wide circle of friends, a gracious, sympathetic wife, and
a fine Concord home featuring a well-stocked library. Emerson was
extremely informative to the young Thoreau, who borrowed the
great man's books, joined his circle of friends, idealized his wife,
and adopted much of his manner and outward appearance.

Thoreau's unconscious imitation of Emerson was so
obvious that other people smiled at it if they were well disposed,
and derided it if not. The following sampler, in which first-time
visitors and old acquaintances alike remark on similarities in voice,
gesture, appearance, habits and even handwriting, could be
replicated several times over.

A fellow graduate of Harvard College, David Green
Haskins, was startled to find Thoreau had so thoroughly absorbed
Emerson's manners, vocal tones, inflections and way of expressing
himself. Haskins had been familiar with Thoreau's voice in college
– "I could have identified him by it in the dark" – and it had borne
no resemblance to Emerson's. Later in Concord, however, Haskins
declared he could not determine, with eyes closed, which of the
two was speaking, and called it "a notable instance of unconscious
imitation." [4]

More facetiously, the author Ednah Littlehale Cheney observed that Thoreau was "all overlaid by an imitation of Emerson; talks like him, puts out his arm like him, brushes his hair in the same way, and is even getting up a caricature nose like Emerson's." [5]

Other contemporaries noticed parallels in wardrobe, and we saw in the previous chapter how cruelly Lowell lampooned Thoreau for derivative literary efforts, throwing in some physical caricature for good measure.

If Thoreau was a pure individualist, though, how could he be such a mimic? Thoreau's admirer Moncure Conway justified the similarities between the two men's expressions and tones thus: "Thoreau was an imitator of no mortal; but Emerson had long been a part of the very atmosphere of Concord, and it was as if this element had deposited on Thoreau a mystical moss." [6]

Ellery Channing, a close companion, leaned toward the same "unconscious" explanation as Haskins and Conway. Channing documents the value that mimicry held for the budding writer. (Thoreau had begun his lifelong journal at Emerson's suggestion, and followed Emerson's practice of treating it as a workbook, later "writing out" – copying or redrafting – useful portions for other works.) "In Emerson's mode of writing out from his Journals, Thoreau imitated him; and yet there was no such thing as conscious imitation in him. His handwriting, too, had such a resemblance to Emerson's that I could hardly tell them apart. It was very strange; for Henry never imitated anybody." [7]

Franklin B. Sanborn, who boarded with the Thoreau family upon settling in Concord in 1855 and knew Henry thereafter, saw "a sort of pocket edition of Mr. Emerson, as far as outward appearance goes... He talks like Mr. Emerson and so spoils the good things which he says; for what in Mr. Emerson is charming, becomes ludicrous in Thoreau, because an imitation." If Sanborn is accurate, a visible mirroring of Emerson evidently persisted well after the two friends broke, if only because it had become second nature. (On the other hand, Sanborn was a late arrival to Concord and a somewhat careless writer, so he could be retailing the gossip of an earlier decade, or could have been influenced by Lowell's verses of 1848.) [8]

"The Arm of an Elm"

Although those with an "as-if" personality give the impression of complete normalcy and, according to Deutsch, are often creatively gifted and bring a clear understanding to intellectual matters, they exclude feelings from their interpersonal contacts. [9]

Many have commented upon Thoreau's lack of warmth. Emerson, remarking on Thoreau's aloofness, commented that taking his friend by the arm was like "taking up the arm of an elm." (JMN 8:498) John Weiss, a classmate at Harvard, found Thoreau "cold and unimpressible," described his handshake as "moist and indifferent," and said that Thoreau seemed to be "living already on some Walden Pond, where he had run up a temporary shanty in the depths of his reserve." [10]

George W. Curtis, author and editor, noted that Thoreau's posture was habitually erect, that he never lounged or slouched, and that he used "a staccato style of speech, every word coming separately and distinctly, as if preserving the same cool isolation in the sentence as [he] did in society ..."

Thoreau's body language reveals the constant tension of one who feels he must be perennially on guard (against himself as well as others). The deliberate and uniform speech pattern that Curtis observed similarly worked as a two-way barrier. Its "cool" tone prevented affect from escaping its inner prison, serving instead a distancing function somewhat like that of a writer's literary style – "but the words were singularly apt and choice," Curtis added, "and Thoreau had always something to say."

At the same time, Thoreau's staccato delivery of novel commentary, by its apparent lack of spontaneity, discouraged any openness or frank dialogue on the part of others. As Curtis pointedly summarizes, "His manner and matter both reproved trifling, but in the most impersonal manner. ... There seemed never to be any loosening of the intellectual tension, and a call [visit] from Thoreau in the highest sense 'meant business.'" [11]

A living example of this compelling effect was Thoreau's correspondent and devoted follower, Harrison Blake, an educator and former clergyman with a bent for Platonic intellectualism that possibly outdid his master's. In a highly interesting apologia for Thoreau's depersonalized social "intercourse," Blake wrote after Thoreau's death:

> Our relation, as I look back on it, seems almost an impersonal one, and illustrates well his remark that 'our thoughts are the epochs in all our lives: all else is but as a journal of the winds that blew while we were here.' ... When together, we had little inclination to talk of personal matters. His aim was directed so steadily and earnestly towards what is essential in our experience, that beyond all others of whom I have known, he made but a single impression on me. Geniality, versatility, personal familiarity are, of course, agreeable in those about us, and seem necessary in human intercourse, but I did not miss them in Thoreau, who was ... such an effectual witness to what is highest and most precious in life. [12]

"An Impenetrable Shield"

The imitative behavior of the "as-if" personality may be considered a defense, analogous to the cuttlefish's inky clouding of the waters (Chapter 10). Although, as we have just seen, Thoreau was described (and described himself) as unemotional, successive biographers have uncovered the particular tenderness that lay at his core. "He was not the cold, unemotional stoic that some have believed, but a warm-blooded human being," wrote Harding, the first authoritative biographer in our time, in 1965. [13] Lebeaux, whose *Young Man Thoreau* (1977) first gave full recognition to the key role played by emotional trauma in Thoreau's life, stated, "It behooves us to see Thoreau as a 'complex and tortured man,' even if this is not what we want to see. He is so complex a man that [biographers'] estimations of his 'happiness' are often wildly at variance." [14]

In the company of contemporaries who knew him well, Thoreau could not long mask his inner vulnerability. Edward Sherman Hoar, a companion on many an amble, believed that Thoreau was concealing "a sensitive and affectionate nature, easily wounded by ... scornful criticism..." Other peers recorded similar observations. [15]

Emerson, however, was a special instance. As an older-generation scion of an established family, Emerson belonged to the Concord aristocracy and moved easily in their circle and that of the elite "Brahmins" of Boston. Aristocratic in personality as well, Emerson was reserved even with loved ones and transcendentalist colleagues, and could be scornful at times. (He once described Thoreau as a "hermit who had retired from the great occasions of life.") Although members of the transcendentalist circle often shared their journal-writings with one another, sharing genuine emotions was an altogether different proposition. Emerson's idealist mind-set and Victorian avoidance of intimacy made him an emotional enigma and, for Thoreau, an ultimately inaccessible father-figure. [16]

Emerson, moreover, tended to delegate a variety of assignments to others, using colleagues as extensions of himself. He considered Bronson Alcott, Margaret Fuller, and Thoreau indispensable companions, as indeed they genuinely were. Their underlying role, according to Joel Porte, was "to keep him on the stretch, provoking him to higher states of thought and feeling." Emerson assimilated the creativity of others, using the fruits of their intellect as a personal resource. [17]

When Thoreau first met Emerson, soon after college, he was trying to consolidate his identity. *"If I am not I, who will be?"* he asked himself. (1:270) For nearly a decade, Emerson provided that identity. When the friendship ultimately chilled, it was because both sensitive souls had too long been "cuttlefish" to one another. On May 24 and 25, 1853, following a particularly aggravating, mutually beclouding encounter, both philosophers made parallel journal entries that reveal how ingrown their identities had become:

Thoreau's Journal	Emerson's Journal
Talked, or tried to talk, with R.W.E. Lost my time – nay, almost my identity. He, assuming a false opposition where there was no difference of opinion, talked to the wind – told me what I knew – and I lost my time trying to imagine myself somebody else to oppose him. (5:188)	H. is military. H. seemed stubborn and implacable; always manly and wise, but rarely sweet. One would say that, as [Daniel] Webster could never speak without an antagonist, so H. does not feel himself except in opposition. He wants a fallacy to expose, a blunder to pillory, requires a little sense of victory, a roll of the drum, to call his powers into full exercise. (JMN 13:183)

Although the Emerson-Thoreau friendship eventually resumed on a quieter basis, the damage was done. "I cannot help counting it a fault that he had no ambition," Emerson orated at his friend's funeral in 1862. "Wanting this, instead of engineering for all America, he was captain of a huckleberry-party." [18]

Yet the relationship needed to be damaged, for it broke Thoreau's long dependency. Discovering his independence in Concord jail and asserting it the next day on Concord's berry-laden hills, Thoreau could put all America behind him, and be his own man. Individualism, one of Thoreau's essential tenets as an adult, cannot co-exist with mirrored behavior.

Thoreau used an analogy from plant life to describe the stifling effect of the state on the individual in "Civil Disobedience." Significantly, it could apply equally well to his relationship with Emerson:

I perceive that, when an acorn and a chestnut fall side by side, the one does not remain inert to make way for the other, but both obey their own laws, and spring and grow and flourish as best they can, till one, perchance, overshadows and destroys the other. If a plant cannot live according to its nature, it dies; and so a man. [19]

After almost dying in the "as-if" mode, Thoreau began living according to his own nature, and became his own man.

12

OTHER PERSONALITY TRAITS

L est it be thought that I only want to pigeon-hole Thoreau's complex, multifaceted personality into the traditional nosological categories of the psychiatrist's bible, the DSM, [1] I wish to affirm categorically that this *erinaceous, vulpine, paradigmatic, heroic, dionysian, apollonian, enigmatic seer* will never be reduced by diagnosis.

The above non-traditional descriptors of Thoreau's salient personality traits are not coinages of mine, nor of psychology. They come from Thoreau and Thoreauvians.

Erinaceous

Thoreau's biographer Harding qualifies him as "the most erinaceous of American writers" because "ideas stuck out from his writings like porcupine quills, guaranteed to prick the hide of even the most thick-skinned. reader." [2]

Attempting to explain his psychic quills, Thoreau wrote:

> *My prickles or smoothness are as much a quality of your hand as of myself. I cannot tell you what I am, more than a ray of the summer's sun. What I am I am, and say not. Being is the great explainer. In the attempt to explain, shall I plane away all the spines, till it is no thistle, but a cornstalk?* (1:222)

Prickles and spines, smoothness and cornstalk (silk?) call to mind Thoreau's "Rough-Smooth" dream (Chapter 4), and it is little wonder that he became more erinaceous during the "Rough" depressed phases of his bipolar disorder.

Another quality of hedgehogs noted by the ancient poet Archilochus: "Fox knows many, / Hedgehog one / Solid trick." [3] Thoreau's solid, infallible trick was self-reform:

When an individual takes a sincere step, then all the gods attend, and his single deed is sweet. (1:247)

Vulpine

Not always erinaceous, Thoreau tracked his quarry in vulpine mode:

I tread in the steps of the fox that has gone before me by some hours, or which perhaps I have started, with such a tip-toe of expectation, as if I were on the trail of the Spirit itself which resides in the wood, and expected soon to catch it in its lair. [4]

The swift-paced, sure-footed hunt was Thoreau's fox-like modus operandi in gathering knowledge for his Kalendar project (Chapter 14):

I soon found myself observing when plants first blossomed and leaved ... running to different sides of the town and into the neighboring towns, often between twenty and thirty miles in a day. (9:158)

It formed the highly therapeutic core of his daily self-treatment throughout his final decade, as we shall see in Chapters 13-16.

Paradigmatic

Like Socrates, Buddha, or Jesus – teachers and examplars – Thoreau has been called paradigmatic. Like them, he often instructed us in parables, from which we might venture to draw precepts. [5]

Also like these sages, Thoreau evolved a transcendent synthesis that reconciles principles commonly thought to be contradictory in order to guide conscientious action in the real world. Consider the contradictory idea of "civil disobedience." The "passive resistance" evidenced in Thoreau's famous jailing for tax refusal is commonly assumed to be rooted in pacifism. Yet a militant spirit underlay his opposition to America's war against Mexico in 1846-48, while his impassioned, controversial defense of John Brown in 1859 praised the abolitionist guerrilla leader's use of violence against evil.

The explanation, according to historians, is that Thoreau's nonviolent "passive resistance" never was rooted in pacifism. As Lawrence Rosenwald emphasizes, "Thoreau criticizes the Mexican War not as a war but as an unjust war; he criticizes not prisons, but unjust imprisonments." As a result, "nonviolence is not a first principle for him; it is at most a practical preference. ... It is ... almost an accident that the essay ["Civil Disobedience"] depicts a nonviolent action."

Rosenwald provides insight into the nature and value of Thoreau's unlikely synthesis:

> To link the Christian pacifism associated with the Quakers to the political liberalism and support for revolution associated with John Locke is indeed a "subtle and ambiguous synthesis"; but it is this synthesis that makes Thoreau's argument useful. It, not the nonresistant rejection of government or coercion generally, is what has mattered to the activist leaders whom Thoreau has influenced.

...And that pragmatic focus on a particular action makes Thoreau's essay legitimately available to sharply opposed readers; both King and Gandhi, on the one hand, and the anonymous fighter in the Danish resistance [for whom "Civil Disobedience" revealed that "nonviolence ... was completely unfit" as a means of resistance against the Gestapo] on the other, are reading Thoreau rightly. [6]

Heroic

Joseph Campbell, in *The Hero With a Thousand Faces* (1949), outlines the destiny of the archetypal hero as told in innumerable mythic variations. The hero (1) ventures forth from the everyday world into one of supernatural wonder; (2) encounters fabulous forces; (3) wins a decisive victory; and finally (4) returns from the mysterious venture bearing a boon to bestow on his fellows in the everyday world. (These steps parallel the sequence of epigenic crises defined by Erik Erikson, which lead to the individual's necessary "psychosocial moratorium" and ultimately to "generativity." [7])

As we have learned, Thoreau's preferred form of storytelling is the excursion, the voyage out and back. Not surprisingly, this pattern is the perfect vehicle of the hero's story. Heroic Thoreau was right indeed to proclaim, *"I have travelled a good deal in Concord."* [8]

1. Leaving home and town and stepping into Walden Woods, Thoreau ventures into a world of supernatural wonders. Gazing at a stand of white pines in sunlight, he is struck by an epiphany, an illumination: *"Certain coincidences like this are accompanied by a certain flash as of hazy lightning, flooding all the world suddenly with a tremulous serene light which is difficult to see long at a time."* (2:107)

2. He encounters such fabulous forces as a loon with a demoniac laughter, *"a long-drawn unearthly howl, probably more like that of a wolf than any bird."* After a zany hour of hide-and-seek, *"he uttered one of those prolonged howls, as if calling on the god of loons to aid him, and* *immediately there came a wind from the east and rippled the surface, and filled the whole air with misty rain, and I was impressed as if it were the prayer of the loon answered, and his god was angry with me; and so I left him disappearing far away on the tumultuous surface."* [9]

3. The hero is victorious and gains special knowledge. As Thoreau announces in the final pages of *Walden*: *"I learned this, at least, by my experiment; that if one advances confidently in the direction of his dreams, and endeavors to live the life which he has imagined, he will meet with a success unexpected in common hours."* [10]

4. He returns among us, bringing the boon of self-reliance, self-reform, simplicity, the *"tonic of wilderness,"* optimism: *"I know of no more encouraging fact than the unquestionable ability of man to elevate his life by a conscious endeavor."* The hero is *"a sojourner in civilized life again."* [11] (See Chapter 16.)

Dionysian

Such persons, like the Greek god of wine, seek intoxication to dispel the ordinary boundaries of existence, trying to become one with the universe through song, dance, intoxicants, etc.

Dionysian Thoreau devised a number of ways to alter consciousness. He listened to the wind in the railroad semaphore, the Aeolian harp, and the wood thrush. Of the latter's song, he wrote: *"I would be drunk, drunk, drunk, dead drunk to this world with it forever ... It, as it were, takes me out of my body and gives me the freedom of all bodies and all nature. I leave my body in a trance and accompany the zephyr and the fragrance."* (6:39-40)

Apollonian

The Apollonian type, says Friedrich Nietzsche, "understands only one law... moderation." Unlike the ego-expanding Dionysian, the tranquil Apollonian observes and contemplates, even though he sings with passion, even amid the frenzy of the dance around him. [12]

Quoting Hindu scripture, Thoreau expressed Apollonian detachment: *"Single is each man born; single he dies; single he receives the reward of his good, and single the punishment of his evil deed."* [13]

Enigmatic

Thoreau, Oates's "supreme poet of doubleness, of evasion and mystery," used the "as-if" trait and "cuttlefish" defense to hide. [14]

Why the evasiveness, the concealment? Thoreau felt vulnerable for at least two reasons that were interrelated, and both connected with Emerson, the man whose life intertwined with his for two decades.

For the older philosopher, as we have seen, Thoreau became a disappointment. Emerson did not appreciate Thoreau's genius, his originality; deciding instead that he lacked ambition; that he never fulfilled his potential to be "engineer for all America." To the contrary, Thoreau sauntered into the wilderness *"to put all America behind him."* The sensitive Thoreau distanced himself from such negative judgments, practicing what Emerson preached.

"And then to think of those I love among men, who will know that I love them though I tell them not!" (2:391) Homoeroticism, no more acceptable in the public mind then than today, was another source of tension. Thoreau understood his differentness; did Emerson sense it, and if so, did he evince discomfort?

No doubt Thoreau's homoeroticism, as Harding writes, "may help to explain some of that sense of guilt which haunts so many of his pages." [15] The person who could confide to his journal, *"the young man is a demigod ... He bathes in light. He is interesting as a stranger from another sphere,"* would need cuttlefish concealment, "as-if" mirroring, and enigma. These were risky feelings to experience in nineteenth-century Concord, let alone to express, even obliquely, even in the pages of a journal. (13:35)

Seer

Like the archetype depicted in the tarot deck, Thoreau may be envisioned as the cloak-clad truth-seeker, leaning on his staff and holding a lamp aloft. Early journalists were fond of comparing Thoreau to Diogenes, the philosopher said to have carried a lamp about in daylight, looking for an honest man. Diogenes, after all, held that virtue is the highest good; self-control the essence of virtue; and love of pleasure for its own sake, evil. [16]

We may imagine Thoreau's cloak as a durable, unpretentious counterstatement to fashion; his staff as the time-annihilating *"world of full and fair proportions"* created by the artist of Kouroo; and his lamp a symbol of the dawn he envisioned. *"To anticipate, not the sunrise and the dawn merely, but, if possible, Nature herself!"* [17]

Dawn-envisioning Thoreau knew himself to be a prophet inspired, a seer. The lone disciples he attracted in his lifetime, like Harrison Blake, sensed the illumination about him. Multi-layered, scriptural *Walden*, the "meditative practice" of writing the late journal in multiple styles, and the hint of ecstasy throughout the pages that came from Thoreau's hand all testify to his visionary calling.

In recent decades, some writers have ventured to see Thoreau in this light. Stanley Cavell, notably, offers a rich discussion of parable-making, prophecy, and the scriptural character of *Walden* in his remarkable reading of that work. Particularly relevant to the theme of the present book, it strikes me, is Cavell's assertion that *Walden's* "wild mood-swings between lamentation and hope" link it to prophetic writings such as those of Hebrew scripture. [18]

13

BATTLE OF THE MIND

Almost two decades after the death of his brother, Thoreau vividly described the challenge posed by his chronic, severe stress disorder:

> *What a battle a man must fight to maintain his standing army of thoughts, and march with them in an orderly array through hostile country. How many enemies there are to sane thinking! A standing army of numerous brave and well-disciplined thoughts, and you at the head of them, marching straight to your goal – how to bring this about is the problem.* [1]

He devised a number of methods to keep his "standing army of thoughts" together, marching them through hostile country (stressful circumstances): attending to sounds (a bird call, the wind playing music upon the semaphore, the chords of the Aeolian harp); practicing yoga; partaking of mystical, meditative, or hallucinatory experiences; writing; and more.

Overall, such practices enabled Thoreau to distract his (thinking) mind with sensory data. Emptied of non-sense, he became sensible, despite the "enemies to sane thinking."

Auditory Stimulation:
"I Leave my Body in a Trance"

Thoreau was exquisitely sensitive to all stimuli, but especially to those of acoustic origin. In the "Sounds" chapter of *Walden*, he referred in ecstatic terms to the tantivy of wild pigeons, the rattle of railroad cars, the bleating of calves and sheep, the bells of Concord and nearby Lincoln, the screech owl, the faraway lowing of a cow, a bullfrog's "trump," and more.

Thoreau, we are told, constructed his own Aeolian harp (a popular stringed mini-harp played by the breeze in an open window). Listening to its infinitely modulated vibrations, or, outdoors, to the breeze passing through the holes of the semaphore's arms, or to the call of the wood thrush (*"the only bird which affects me like music"*), he declared:

> *He that hath ears, let him hear. The contact of sound with a human ear whose hearing is pure and unimpaired is coincident with an ecstasy. ... It, as it were, takes me out of my body and gives me the freedom of all bodies and all nature. I leave my body in a trance and accompany the zephyr and the fragrance.* (6:39-40)

Thoreau made therapeutic use of music in periods of deep emotional disruption. During his brother's fatal illness, a music box conveyed *"the beauty and harmony of the universe."* Following a particularly grisly reminder of mortality on the eleventh anniversary of John's death, the wind playing music upon the semaphore once *"intoxicate*[d]*"* him and *"made* [him] *sane."*

Similarly, on the fifteenth anniversary, Thoreau in the midst of despair found the ego-dissolving strains of music restorative:

> *What is there in music that it should so stir our deeps? We are all ordinarily in a state of desperation; such is our life; ofttimes it drives us to suicide. To how many, perhaps to most, life is barely tolerable, and if it were not for the fear of death or of dying, what a multitude would immediately commit suicide! But let us hear a strain of music, we are at once advertised of a life which no man had told us of, which no preacher preaches. Suppose I try to describe faithfully the prospect which a strain of music exhibits to me. The field of my life becomes a boundless plain, glorious to tread, with no death or disappointment at the end of it. All meanness and*

*trivialness disappear. I become adequate to any deed. No
particulars survive this expansion; persons do not survive it.
In the light of this strain there is no thou or I. We are
actually lifted above ourselves.* (9:222)

Acoustic stimuli in Thoreau's workaday world could alter
his consciousness, lifting him to the same transcendent plane:

*When my hoe tinkled against the stones, that music echoed
to the woods and the sky, and was an accompaniment to
my labor which yielded an instant and immeasurable crop.
It was no longer beans that I hoed, nor I that hoed beans;
and I remembered with as much pity as pride, if I
remembered at all, my acquaintances who had gone to the
city to attend the oratorios.* 2 *

Finally, Thoreau found transcendence in the making of
actual music as well:

*When I play my flute to-night, earnest as if to leap the
bounds [of] the narrow fold where human life is penned,
and range the surrounding plain, I hear echo from a
neighboring wood, a stolen pleasure occasionally not
rightfully heard, much more for other ears than ours, for 'tis
the reverse of sound. It is not our own melody that comes
back to us, but an amended strain. And I would only hear
myself as I would hear my echo, corrected and repronounced
for me. It is as when my friend reads my verse.* (1:375)

---

* This calls to mind a comment by the remarkable American composer
Charles Ives (whose "Concord" piano sonata includes a "Thoreau"
movement): "Thoreau was a great musician, not because he played the
flute but because he did not have to go to Boston to hear 'the
Symphony.'" ("Thoreau: Nature's Musician," 1920, in Harding, *A Profile*,
105.

Psychoactive Substances:
"You Go Beyond the Furthest Star"

Intrigued by a variety of psychoactive substances, Thoreau read about them, described their mind-altering effects, and partook of at least one, once. For example, finding himself "*becalmed in the infinite leisure and repose of nature*" under a noonday sun, and consequently fantasizing about Asian "*lands of contemplation*," Thoreau praised the "*luxury of idleness*" and thought he "*could find some apology even for the instinct of the opium, betel, and tobacco chewers.*"

Citing a naturalist-traveller of whom he had read, Thoreau described a tree that grows on a mountain in what is now Yemen: "'*The soft tops of the twigs and tender leaves are eaten,*' says his reviewer, '*and produce an agreeable soothing excitement, restoring from fatigue, banishing sleep, and disposing to the enjoyment of conversation.*'" [4]

When Thoreau underwent dental surgery in 1851, the ether administered to him left a lasting impression. (The anesthetic was first used in medicine in the 1840s.) Thoreau wrote:

> By taking the ether the other day I was convinced how far asunder a man could be separated from his senses. You are told that it will make you unconscious, but no one can imagine what it is to be unconscious — how far removed from the state of consciousness and all that we call this world — until he has experienced it. The value of the experiment is that it does give you experience of an interval as between one life and another, — a greater space than you ever travelled. You are a sane mind without organs, — groping for organs,— which if it did not soon recover its old senses would get new ones. You expand like a seed in the ground. You exist in your roots, like a tree in the winter. If you have an inclination to travel, take the ether; you go beyond the furthest star. (2:194) [5]

Intrigued as Thoreau may have been with other people's reports of the "elevating" effects of certain drugs, this single, supervised encounter with ether seems to have been the extent of his own experience with any. He would refuse opiates on his deathbed in 1862, "declaring uniformly that he preferred to endure with a clear mind the worst penalties of suffering, rather than be plunged in a turbid dream of narcotics." [6]

Mysticism: "I Am a Restless Kernel in the Magazine of the Universe"

"*I am a mystic*," was the way Thoreau introduced himself to the Association for the Advancement of Science. By mystic, he referred to feelings of oneness in the universe that he sought and sometimes attained:

> *If with closed ears and eyes I consult consciousness for a moment, immediately are all walls and barriers dissipated, earth rolls from under me, and I float, by the impetus derived from the earth and the system, a subjective, heavily laden thought, in the midst of an unknown and infinite sea, or else heave and swell like a vast ocean of thought, without rock or headland, where are all riddles solved, all straight lines making there their two ends to meet, eternity and space gambolling familiarly through my depths. I am from the beginning, knowing no end, no aim. No sun illumines me, for I dissolve all lesser lights in my own intenser and steadier light. I am a restful kernel in the magazine of the universe.* (1:53-54)

He achieved his mystical states through music, and also used meditation and yoga.

Meditation and Yoga:
"I Grew …like Corn in the Night"

In his meditative practices, Thoreau focused on the sensuous – what he could touch, taste, hear, see, feel – as in the often-remarked passage in *Walden*:

> *Sometimes, in a summer morning, having taken my accustomed bath, I sat in my sunny doorway from sunrise till noon, rapt in a revery, amidst the pines and hickories and sumachs, in undisturbed solitude and stillness, while the birds sang around … until by the sun falling in at my west window, or the noise of some traveller's wagon on the distant highway, I was reminded of the lapse of time. I grew in those seasons like corn in the night, and they were far better than any work of the hands would have been.* [7]

Thoreau enjoyed this ego-less state. Not surprisingly, Icarian imagery came to mind, as well as Hindu lore, when he depicted meditation:

> *Free in this world, as the birds in the air, disengaged from every kind of chains, those who have practiced the yoga gather in the Brahma the certain fruit of their works. Depend upon it that rude and careless as I am, I would fain practice the* yoga *faithfully.* [8]

By such faithful, self-reliant practices, Thoreau lived a meditative lifestyle, which he saw as the treatment of choice for a severe stress disorder.

14

THE KALENDAR PROJECT

*Though I knew most of the flowers, and there were not in
any particular swamp more than half a dozen shrubs that I
did not know, yet these made it seem like a maze to me...*
—Journal (9:157)

Plagued by mood swings from childhood and afflicted, as we
have seen, with seasonal ("November eat-heart") depression,
Thoreau around 1860-61 became powerfully possessed by a
cyclical interest that he had been pursuing for a decade. He was
now completely persuaded, after years of intimacy with the cycles
and rhythms of his natural environment, that these cycles were
identical to those he sensed within himself:

> *These regular phenomena of the seasons get at last to be —
> they were at first, of course — simply and plainly phenomena
> or phases of my life. The seasons and all their changes are
> in me. ... Almost I believe the Concord would not rise and
> overflow its banks again, were I not here. After a while I
> learn what my moods and seasons are. I would have
> nothing subtracted. I can imagine nothing added. My
> moods are thus periodical, not two days in my year alike.
> The perfect correspondence of Nature to man, so that he is
> at home in her!* (10:127; Thoreau's emphasis)

A Page from Thoreau's Kalendar

To map the cyclical aspects of natural phenomena, Thoreau devised a great number of charts using this format. The columns were years (completed cycles), the rows were categories of phenomena. Thoreau sorted the data from years of field notes into these grids. Each chart was dedicated to one category of phenomena and occupied several oversize sheets, about 15x17 inches. This is the first sheet of a chart titled "Earliest Flowering of April Flowers," about 1860.

(Morgan Library)

It seemed to Thoreau that he might mine the mass of scientific data he had accumulated in his journal – the result of years of nature observation – and fashion a structure, a framework that would articulate all natural cycles and thereby help to stabilize his emotional highs and lows. He began to create his Kalendar.*

Thoreau scholar Bradley Dean has summarized Thoreau's intent with rich concision:

> Apparently he intended to write a comprehensive history of the natural phenomena that took place in his hometown each year. Although he planned to base his natural history of Concord upon field observations recorded in his journal over a period of several years, he would synthesize those observations so that he could construct a single "archetypal" year, a technique he had used to wonderful effect in *Walden*. The observations he recorded in his journal ranged from the most purely objective and scientific to the aesthetic and highly subjective. He would supplement his own wide-ranging observations in his "Kalendar" project...with extracts from his extensive reading. [1]

Thus, with the journal observations as raw material, Thoreau expected to forge a synthesis of the inner and outer worlds – transcending the usual dichotomy between the "purely objective and scientific" and the "aesthetic and highly subjective." But before the writing work could begin, the writer would have to complete his preliminary labors: the outlining, the plotting, the organization of phenomena by category and date – listing, mapping, charting.

---

* The Kalendar had been a longstanding idea, in one form or another. Five years earlier (1852) he had written: "*Why should I hear the chattering of blackbirds, why smell the skunk each year? I would fain explore the mysterious relation between myself and these things. I would at least know what these things unavoidably are, make a chart of our life, know how its shores trend, that buttterflies reappear and when, why just this circle of creatures completes the world.*" (3:438).

This is where Icarus, fallen into the sea (or *"any particular swamp"*), calls upon Daedalus, architect and master of the labyrinth, to lead him out of the swamp-maze and restore him to solid ground, to life and generativity.

If Thoreau would know his cycles, his circles, his spirals, he must first draw lines, rectangles, boxes – a grid, a chart with a horizontal and vertical axis – on paper. (He used oversized sheets.)

Initially, these blank forms for chart-making might represent the discouraging "maze" he refers to in this chapter's epigraph – until he can fill in the squares with every last flower and shrub (and *"birds and whatever else might offer"*), that is, until he has recorded every seasonal cycle and can grasp them in their interconnected wholeness. Then, the writing can begin.

And so, in a surge of generativity around 1861 (the last calendar-year of his life), Thoreau prepared his Kalendar as a huge master-chart. On page after page, he sorted his data into the grids. The columns were years (completed cycles), the rows were categories of phenomena. Sometimes entire charts were devoted to the amount of rainfall; amount of snowfall; opening of leaves or flowers; wildlife migrations; water levels and temperatures; wind force, etc.

Throughout the 1850s, it had been Thoreau's habit to traverse over a hundred miles of countryside weekly, in all weathers, recording field observations and meticulous measurements in virtually every ecological niche in the Concord environment. In the course of these repeated excursions, he realized what else (or whom else) he was seeking. As he wrote in his journal, he wished to anticipate his moods by correlating them with natural happenings: *"I would know when in the year to expect thoughts and moods, as the sportsman knows when to look for plover."* (12:347) The assumption was that, as a creature of nature, by knowing what to expect about bird, shrub, and beetle, he could better predict and control his own affect.

On the run every day to discover and observe, fox-like Thoreau kept in tune, informed, and limber:

I often visited a particular plant four or five miles distant, half a dozen times within a fortnight, that I might know exactly when it opened, beside attending to a great many others in different directions and some of them equally distant, at the same time. At the same time I had an eye for birds and whatever else might offer. (9:158)

"*I wanted to know my neighbors, if possible – to get a little nearer to them,*" Thoreau wrote of these exhaustive excursions. By getting nearer, he felt he would be better in touch with, and be better able to change his inner environment. At the outset of his project, he had exclaimed: "*Ah! ... that I could match nature always with my moods! that in each season when some part of nature especially flourishes, then a corresponding part of me may not fail to flourish !*" (2:391)

Thoreau would then make a conscious effort to become part of all that he touched, tasted, smelled, saw, or heard: "*Live in each season as it passes,*" he admonished others as he did himself:

... breathe the air, drink the drink, taste the fruit, and resign yourself to the influences of each. Let them be your only diet drink and botanical medicines. In August live on berries ... Grow green with spring, yellow and ripe with autumn. Drink of each season's influence as a vial, a true panacea of all remedies, mixed for your especial use. (5:394)

"*Nature,*" he asserted, "*is but another name for health.*" [2] And in *Walden*: "*For my panacea, instead of one of those quack vials ..., let me have a draught of undiluted morning air.*" [3]

Joel Porte, in his discussion of Thoreau's sensuous life, on which this chapter relies, states: "Thoreau's outlook was strongly dependent on the life of the senses." [4] Indeed, it could be said that Thoreau's mental health depended on his sensuous life: "*To see the sun rise or go down every day would preserve us sane forever,– so to relate ourselves, for our mind's and body's health, to a universal fact.*" (3:208)

Perhaps by sublimating his *sensual* life, his *sensuous* life became more vivid. In any case, Thoreau declared, "*There can be no* *really black melan-choly to him who lives in the midst of nature and has still his senses."* (1:364) * The Kalendar master chart enabled him to equilibrate the black melan-cholic depressions with the sky-blue Icarian manic flights, and achieve euthymia.

As Thoreau sat at the wall-corner, high on Conantum one afternoon in October, 1857, suddenly a low-slanted glade of intense, pure-white light fell on a grove of bare gray maples, lighting them up. Every recess was filled and lit up with this pure white light. Reflecting on the maples far down the stream, Thoreau wrote: *I dreamed I walked like a liberated spirit in their maze."* (10:133) The Kalendar project enabled him to live out his dream, and transcend his Daedalian maze.

---

* Thoreau hyphenates "melancholy" in the journal, probably to accentuate the literal meaning ("black bile").

15

WRITING IT OUT

Writing was a crucial part of the treatment program that Thoreau unconsciously devised to deal with his severe stress, mood and personality disorders. "One of the functions of Thoreau's writing," Robert Sayre notes,

> was a kind of private therapy. It provided an arena in which he could defend himself and counter the attacks of his townsmen. It was a setting in which to meditate and continue to absorb the therapeutic influences of nature. It was a perfect complement to his walks and his solitude. [1]

Thoreau, we have seen, veiled the nature of his first major writing project:

> *My purpose in going to Walden Pond was not to live cheaply nor to live dearly there, but to transact some private business with the fewest obstacles; to be hindered from accomplishing which for want of a little common sense, a little enterprise and business talent, appeared not so sad as foolish.* [2]

The *"obstacles"* that Thoreau needed to minimize were the everyday travails of earning a living. The *"private business"* was the work of grieving and mourning the most important person in Thoreau's life.

As noted in Chapter 1, Thoreau accomplished a degree of mourning-work by drafting a memoir with undertones of an elegy or memorial, *A Week on the Concord and Merrimack Rivers*. The writing and architecture of *A Week* were critical tools in Thoreau's grief-work. "The trip [on the rivers] took two weeks; his account of that trip occupied Thoreau on and off for ten years, nearly a quarter of his lifetime," as Linck C. Johnson, the leading *Week* expert, emphasizes. While this "private" business was transacted, Thoreau attended to early drafts of parts of the book that became *Walden*, an account of his psychospiritual rebirth. [3]

Leaving his pond-side house one day in July 1846 to pick up a mended shoe in town, Thoreau wound up in jail for nonpayment of taxes. His choice of incarceration over compliance – an act of historic consequence, as we know today – provoked only bafflement and blame at the time, even among those who might be expected to sympathize. Thoreau's brief jail experience – or, speaking psychiatrically, the need he soon felt to defend his misunderstood behavior by writing it out – generated another critical writing project conceived during Thoreau's sojourn at Walden Pond. [4]

By the time Thoreau left the woods, after a sojourn of two years, two months and two days, he had two major works in progress – *A Week* and *Walden* – voluminous journal pages, including material for other future essays, and the idea of writing up a public lecture on "the Rights and Duties of the Individual in Relation to Government," later printed as the essay "Resistance to Civil Government," better known as "Civil Disobedience."

A Week: Ambivalence and Unexpressed Grief

On the last day of August, 1839, Henry and John Thoreau took a vacation from their teaching duties at the Concord Academy. They outfitted their homemade rowboat, the "Musketaquid," with a sail, equipment, and supplies, and traveled down the Concord and up the Merrimack River into New Hampshire. On the slow-flowing Concord, Thoreau would later write, "*we seemed to be embarked on the placid current of our dreams, floating from past to future as silently as one awakes to fresh morning or evening thoughts.*" [5]

In the placid current of their dreams, the brothers may well have floated on the love they felt for one another. The rivalrous love they both felt for Ellen Sewall, the lovely young woman we met in our opening chapter, troubled those currents.

As we saw in the Prologue, the siblings' rivalry was all the more intensely felt for being largely unspoken. Henry, who wanted Ellen for his own, must certainly have wanted John out of the way. Psychologically, the rivalry set the stage for guilt and recurrent depression after John's untimely death. When Henry survived John's death (and he almost did not), he felt a heavy burden of guilt.

One year following the death – conceivably experiencing memories of both John and Ellen – Thoreau concluded his first published reform essay with an idealization of love as the source of self-reform (*"a paradise within"*).

> *Love is the wind, the tide, the waves, the sunshine. Its power is incalculable; it is many horse power. It never ceases, it never slacks; it can move the globe without a resting-place; it can warm without fire; it can feed without meat; it can clothe without garments; it can shelter without roof. It can make a paradise within[,] which will dispense with a paradise without.* [6]

Henry's intense ambivalence toward John is reflected in the constrained form he chose to memorialize his death. As mentioned earlier, *A Week* is the prose equivalent of the elegy, a poem in which the name of the deceased is never mentioned. As readers, we never see the living, active John of the 1839 excursion; he speaks no words, has no name; we are never assured of his reality. John does not really function as an individual character in Thoreau's narrative, despite the occasional first person plural pronoun. [7]

Intense ambivalence disrupts the normal process of grieving. This can cause a situation in which the grief remains unexpressed; as a result, the deceased remains alive and well (figuratively speaking) in the survivor. This was the case with Thoreau. As previously observed, Thoreau internalized his idealized brother as his ego-ideal.

Thoreau recorded in *A Week* a pertinent image of unexpressed grief, reflecting his own psychic functioning: *"Like some*

Indian tribes, we bear about with us the mouldering relics of our ancestors on our shoulders." [8]

The mouldering relics slid from his shoulders into Thoreau's prose as he wrote out multiple versions of his archetypal confrontations with death's finality. This is evident in *Cape Cod*, where Thoreau presents the Atlantic shore – the scene of frequent shipwrecks – as *"a vast* morgue... *The carcasses of men and beasts together lie stately up upon its shelf, rotting and bleaching in the sun and waves, and each tide turns them in their beds, and tucks fresh sand under them."* Despite comic relief, Thoreau's underlying vision in *Cape Cod* is morbid from its very first pages, which describe the aftermath of the fatal wreck of the "St. John." (Did the ship's name, identical to that of his "saintly" brother, help trigger Thoreau's response?) [9]

Walden: Death and Psychospiritual Rebirth

Death and dying figure significantly in *Walden*, but in the cyclic context of purification and rebirth. "The whole of *Walden*," Hyman notes, "runs to symbols of graves and coffins, with consequent rising from them." Decay fertilizes, and *Walden* explores "every phase and type of decay: rotting ice, decaying trees, moldy pitch pine and rotten wood, excrement, maggots, a vulture feeding on a dead horse, carrion, tainted meat, and putrid water." [10]

Death was a preoccupation, and Thoreau could rouse himself from the most morbid depressions by returning to the idea that all living beings – notably, he and his brother – were part of nature's endless cycles, and that nothing ever dies: *"The earth is not a mere fragment of dead history, ... but living poetry ... not a fossil earth, but a living earth..."* Since earth's fecundity is increased by decay, *"our human life but dies down to its roots and still puts forth its green blade to eternity."* [11]

On one wintry day, Thoreau described a crust of snow by Walden Pond and commented that there was a similar crust of snow over his heart. At spring's approach – with his writing-it-out therapy, Kalendar project, yoga, music, meditation and other consciousness-altering techniques – Thoreau was able to signal a change in himself that he always knew was coming: *"...winter breaks up within us; the frost is coming out of me, and I am heaved like the road; accumulated masses of ice and snow dissolve, and thoughts like a freshet pour down unwonted channels."* (5:34)

Having sloughed the mouldering ancestral relics off his shoulders, Thoreau could attend to his rebirth. With the thawing of Walden Pond, his alter ego, he was able to proclaim: *"Walden was dead and is alive again."* [12]

"Civil Disobedience": A Counter-Frictional Life

When Thoreau came into town to pick up his mended shoe, he met his acquaintance and sometime surveying client Sam Staples, Concord's jailkeeper and constable, who sympathetically warned him that his tax delinquency of several years would land him in jail he could not find a solution. After spending his now-famous night in Concord's whitewashed jail cell, Thoreau proceeded to the shoemaker's to complete his interrupted errand, then went off to lead a group of huckleberry-gatherers in the hills as he had promised – *"and in half an hour ... was in the midst of a huckleberry field, on one of our highest hills, two miles off, and then the State was nowhere to be seen."* [13]

Out of this experience came the essay "Civil Disobedience," the first and doubtless the most consequential justification ever written of the right to resist unjust laws on the basis of individual conscience.

At the time that it happened, however, the meaning of Thoreau's all-but-unprecedented act of civil disobedience eluded nearly everyone in town – it seemed just another example of his outlandish behavior, like the Walden Woods fire. Even those who might have taken Thoreau's side evidently deserted him.

The aristocratic and cautious Emerson was deeply scandalized by his disciple's seeming flirtation with common criminality. Joel Porte points out an emotional factor surely influencing Emerson's negative judgment at this particular point in the two men's careers: "Thoreau represented the side of Emerson – rebellious, unsocial, brooding, in love with artistic 'idleness' – which the older man increasingly came to dislike and wished to suppress." [14]

To Bronson Alcott, another Concord transcendentalist who was close to both of them, Emerson complained that Thoreau's action was "mean and skulking, and in bad taste." Alcott was the town's only other example of a tax resister, having been arrested, though not jailed, three years earlier for nonpayment. He replied in defense of what he called "dignified non-compliance with the injunction of civil powers." [15] Emerson, not persuaded, wrote in his journal a bit of cautionary advice, as if speaking to Thoreau:

> The State is a poor, good beast who means the best: it means friendly. A poor cow who does well by you,– do not grudge it its hay. ... As long as the state means you well, do not refuse your pistareen [coin] ... The prison is one step to suicide.

In sum, he cautioned Thoreau, "Do not run amok against society." (JMN 9:446)

Shame and Pride

One of Thoreau's earliest journal entries, at age 21, deals with the challenge of finding some meaningful and dignified conduit for his energies:

> *What may a man do and not be ashamed of it? ... Such is man,– toiling, heaving, struggling ant-like to shoulder some stray unappropriated crumb and deposit it in his granary; ... Can he not, wriggling, screwing, self-exhorting, self-constraining, wriggle or screw out something that shall live,– respected, intact, intangible, not to be sneezed at?* (1:34-35). *

---

* Note the use of Daedalian imagery.

Emerson, bigger than the ant, was not only sneezing at his disciple's unashamed, respectable, intact effort to forge "*something that shall live*," but admonishing him that this choice of prison was a step toward self-inflicted death. More than probably, Thoreau felt mortified that his high-minded moral behavior was thus deprecated by his friend and mentor.

In his early twenties, Thoreau had set down a code of conduct to take advantage of adversity:

> *Make the most of your regrets; never smother your sorrow, but tend and cherish it till it come to have a separate and integral interest. To regret deeply is to live afresh. By so doing you will be astonished to find yourself restored to all your emoluments.* (1:95)

In middle age, three years before his death, Thoreau revealed a facet of his personality that he usually concealed:

> *How much the writer lives and endures in coming before the public so often ! A few years or books are with him equal to a long life of experience, suffering, etc. It is well if he does not become hardened. He learns how to bear contempt...* (11:452)

Writing was the chief way Thoreau sought to "*make the most of [his] regrets*," but he did not find his early efforts restorative. Quite early in his journal-keeping, he wanted to know, "*what does all this scribbling amount to?*"

> *What is now scribbled in the heat of the moment one can contemplate with somewhat of satisfaction, but alas ! to-morrow – aye, tonight – it is stale, flat, and unprofitable,– in fine, is not, only its shell remains...* (1:34)

Gradually, this maturing Hamlet learned to transform his scribbling into creations fit to join "*the treasured wealth of the world and the fit inheritance of generations and nations,"* as he said of enduring books in Walden. [17]

When he composed the final version of "Civil Disobedience" for publication nearly three years following his incarceration, Thoreau brought the injustice of slavery in America to the foreground of his argument. Thoreau's scathing commentary on his country's pro-slavery war against Mexico produced the memorable, rousing declarations of a conscientious objector. As is well known, "Civil Disobedience" became, over time, the founding document of resistance philosophies that have ranged from individual noncompliance to organized mass action.

For those who might recognize it, *Walden* contains an explicit rejoinder to Emerson's long-echoing advice, when Thoreau briefly refers to his prison episode:

> *It is true, I might have resisted forcibly with more or less effect, might have run "amok" against society; but I preferred that society should run "amok" against me, it being the desperate party.* [18]

Justifying his passive resistance despite Emerson's deprecations, Thoreau had found *"what a man may do and not be ashamed of it."* Astonished, he found himself restored, and has become humankind's perennial restorer.

"Let your life be a counter friction to stop the machine," Thoreau admonished in "Civil Disobedience." He referred to the machinery of government in the service of injustice, but the idea could also apply to human relations. Against the trivial, inauthentic and stifling machinations of others, Thoreau made his life a counter-friction. [19]

Botanical Language Applied:
A Flower's Leaf and Human Flowering

How copious and precise the botanical language to describe the leaves, as well as the other parts of the plant! ... It is wonderful how much pains has [sic] been taken to describe a flower's leaf, compared for instance with the care that is taken in describing a psychological fact.

... We are armed with language adequate to describe each leaf in the field, or at least to distinguish it from each other, but not to describe a human character. Journal (2:409-10)

Thoreau began botanizing in earnest in 1851. In that year, the journal swelled to new proportions as he now used it to record detailed, daily field observations in additional to his philosophical and literary comments. In a famous journal entry, Thoreau described his new approach of *"attending to plants with more method,"* gathering specimens every day in an increasingly decrepit straw hat, and mastering botanical nomenclature and scientific classification. Most importantly, he paid frequent visits to specific sites to track a certain plant's unfoldings, to know its cycles.

At first (Thoreau wrote), he contemplated meeting the challenge in Daedalian fashion:

> *I remember gazing with interest at the swamps about those days and wondering if I could ever attain to such familiarity with plants that I should know the species of every twig and leaf in them, that I should be acquainted with every plant (excepting grasses and cryptogamous ones), summer and winter, that I saw. Though I knew most of the flowers, and there were not in any particular swamp more than half a dozen shrubs that I did not know, yet these made it seem* like a maze to me, *of a thousand strange species, and I even thought of commencing at one end and looking it faithfully and laboriously through till I knew it all. I little thought that in a year or two I should have attained to that knowledge without all that labor.* (9:157; my emphasis)

Thoreau managed this feat of omniscience, he wrote, not by systematic rules of study (*"the most natural system is still so artificial"*), but instead by throwing himself totally into a pursuit * − a daily regimen combining sustained muscular exercise, intense sensory stimulation, obsessive record-keeping, and an Icarian celerity.

> *I soon found myself observing when plants first blossomed and leafed, and I followed it up early and late, far and near, several years in succession, running to different sides of the town and into the neighboring towns, often between twenty and thirty miles in a day. I often visited a particular plant four or five miles distant, half a dozen times within a fortnight, that I might know exactly when it opened, beside attending to a great many others in different directions and some of them equally distant, at the same time. At the same time I had an eye for birds and whatever else might offer.* (9:157)

Thoreau was not facetious when, in the epigraph that opens this chapter, he envisioned characterizing human psychology with the expressive exactitude of botanical language. It is extraordinarily significant that, at this crucial life-season of transition and maturation, Thoreau came into his true calling by attaining such a degree of community, such empathy, with plant life. Now he would write this out.

Quoting seven detailed descriptions in a recent manual by the botanist and evolutionist Asa Gray, Thoreau elaborated upon each passage, drawing extended parallels with human psychological development. Thoreau thus substantiated the important concept that the "ethereal" world of ideas is grounded in the natural world. For several journal pages, he elaborated on the *"perfect analogy"* he saw *"between the life of the human being and that of the vegetable, both of the body and the mind."* (2:201) For example, he cites Gray as follows:

> "Roots not only spring from the root-end of the primary stem in germination, but also from any subsequent part of the stem under favorable

---

* As mentioned in Chapter 12, "Vulpine."

circumstances, that is to say, in darkness and moisture, as when covered by the soil or resting on its surface."

Thoreau then comments:

No thought but is connected as strictly as a flower, with the earth. The mind flashes not so far on one side but its rootlets, its spongelets, find their way instantly on the other side into a moist darkness, uterine,— a low bottom in the heavens, even miasma-exhaling to such immigrants as are not acclimated. A cloud is uplifted to sustain its roots. Imbosomed in clouds as in a chariot, the mind drives through the boundless fields of space. Even there is the dwelling of Indra. (2:204-05)

In another example, Thoreau cites Gray on the varieties of root-formation:

"They [roots] may even strike in the open air and light, as is seen in the copious aërial rootlets by which the Ivy, the Poison Ivy, and the Trumpet Creeper climb and adhere to the trunks of trees or other bodies; and also in Epiphytes or Air-plants, of most warm regions, which have no connection whatever with the soil, but germinate and grow high in air on the trunks or branches of trees, etc.; as well as in some terrestrial plants, such as the Banian and Mangrove, that send off aërial roots from their trunks or branches, which finally reach the ground."

To this, Thoreau adds his own conclusion:

So, if our light-and-air-seeking tendencies extend too widely for our original root or stem, we must send downward new roots to ally us to the earth. (2:205)

Thoreau's glosses on Gray, far beyond the literary exercise of metaphor-making, were therapeutic activities. Connecting heaven and earth, cloud and roots, aerial and subterranean, sunlight and darkness, they enabled bipolar Thoreau to maintain a balance between Icarian and Daedalian traits, and achieve euthymia.

16

A Monarch Surveys

We should make our notch every day on our characters, as
Robinson Crusoe on his stick. (1:220)

The innovative methods that Thoreau devised to stabilize moods, relieve stress, and become his own man enhanced one another.

Consider, for example, the insight he derived from plant study: *"...if our light-and-air-seeking tendencies extend too widely for our original root or stem, we must send downward new roots to ally us to the earth."* (2:205)

The Kalendar project enabled bipolar Thoreau to predict when the Icarian *"light-and-air-seeking tendencies* [would) *extend too widely"* so that, as Daedalus, he could send new roots earthward to ground himself.

The healing sounds of music, we have seen, brought a spiritual oneness: *"In the light of this strain* [of music] *there is no thou or I."* (9:222) Heavenly music lifted Daedalian Thoreau from a cognitive maze.

Surveying – the outdoor profession that exercised so many of Thoreau's skills and earned him a living – helped ground high-flying Icarus.

Grounding himself with active botanizing, healing music, yoga, meditation, writing-it-out, the Kalendar project, and surveying (property bounds, *"forest paths and all across-lot routes,"* nature and human nature), Thoreau mastered his mental kingdom, like that successful castaway and literary icon of solitude, Robinson Crusoe.

It is Crusoe whom Thoreau essentially cited in *Walden* when expounding the benefits of virtual, not actual, land ownership. "*With respect to landscapes*," he wrote,

> I am monarch of all I *survey*,
> My right there is none to dispute. [1]

Those are the opening lines of William Cowper's "Verses supposed to be written by Alexander Selkirk" (1782). The real-life Selkirk, Defoe's model for Robinson Crusoe, survived alone on an island off Chile for four years and four months.

Thoreau and Selkirk had this in common: in their self-exiles, they both encountered traumatic stressors that could have destroyed them. Both availed themselves of their solitude in nature, explored and mastered their mental kingdoms, and emerged from the wilderness as monarchs.

Epilogue:

A Winged Life and the Artist's Staff

Thoreau, who loved parables and fables, told an Icarian folk tale on the last page of *Walden:*

> Every one has heard the story which has gone the rounds of New England, of a strong and beautiful bug which came out of the dry leaf of an old table of apple-tree wood, which had stood in a farmer's kitchen for sixty years... from an egg deposited in the living tree many years earlier still... which was heard gnawing out for several weeks, hatched perchance by the heat of an urn.

Following his near-death encounter from facsimile lockjaw, the psychic numbing of PTSD, and continuous mood swings, Thoreau's battered, defended ego could be compared to the insect's *"beautiful and winged life ... buried for ages [in] its well-seasoned tomb,"* a fertile egg probably sealed off from all chance of hatching.

Yet by assembling his Kalendar project, altering his mood and awareness with the Aeolian harp and the wood thrush song, and writing out his grief, anger, self-defenses and raptures., Thoreau enabled his winged life to emerge from *"many concentric layers of woodenness in the dead dry life of society ... to enjoy its perfect summer at last."* [1]

"I Am Time and the World"

One measure of Thoreau's success at self-healing may be inferred from his evolving concepts of time.

Thoreau's preoccupation with time is evident from the first page of his lifelong journal, which he subtitled: *"Gleanings or What Time Has Not Reaped From My Journal."*

In the very first entry, Thoreau describes the state of solitude as an escape from the conditions of time and selfhood: *"To be alone I find it necessary to escape the present,– I avoid myself."* (1:3)

Thoreau's reflections on music express an idea of time as more than a linear flow – as a web or fabric whose weave connects the present with antiquity and universalizes human experience:

> *Of what manner of stuff is the web of time wove, when these consecutive sounds called a strain of music can be wafted down through centuries from Homer to me, and Homer have been conversant with that same unfathomable mystery and charm which so newly tingles my ears?* (1:316-17)

What is linear here is not historical time itself, but time's content – a "strain" (strand, line, lineage) of "consecutive sounds" which, Thoreau seems to imply, symbolizes or actually is one of the innumerable threads in the weave of time.

The continuity of time, however conceived, was profoundly disrupted by John's death. Two and a half months following it, Thoreau wrote: *"How near is yesterday ! How far tomorrow ! I have seen nails which were driven before I was born. Why do they look old and rusty? Why does not God make some mistake to show to us that time is a delusion? Why did I invent time but to destroy it?"* (1:349)

He tried, unsuccessfully at first, to restore the torn fabric, the broken thread, his disrupted oneness with time's weave. The web of time was the matrix of life and death, birth and destruction. Insofar as time, infinite and cyclical, was the weave that universalizes human experience, it was the vehicle of his identity: *"I am time and the world,"* he proclaimed in the same passage. Like God or Brahma, he could declare: *"...In me are summer and winter, village life and commercial routine, pestilence and famine and refreshing breezes, joy and sadness, life and death."* (1:349)

Later, in *Walden*, Thoreau would devise a new metaphor. Time was a line, but not the conventional line of chronology.

Rather, the line is the infinitely thin separator between the past and the future. It is the present, the very point he once sought to escape – the infinitesimal moment that is practically impossible to dwell in, the point where it is the seer's duty to stand. Thus he tells us he is *"anxious to improve the nick of time ... to stand on the meeting of two eternities, the past and future, which is precisely the present moment; to toe that line."* [2] In another linear-flow metaphor, he differentiates the passage of time from its eternal content, which he seeks: *"Time is but the stream I go a-fishing in."* [3]

An Artist's Staff

In his conclusion to *Walden,* Thoreau invents the parable of an artist who took time to fashion a staff of wood – not an everyday staff on which to nick notches marking the passage of chronological time, but a perfect creation that abolishes time – for time does not enter into a perfect work. *"As he made no compromise with Time,"* Thoreau writes, *"Time kept out of his way..."* After the passage of countless millennia – *"Brahma had awoke and slumbered countless times"* – the staff is at last perfectly crafted. Suddenly, Thoreau tells us, it *"expanded before the eyes of the astonished artist into the fairest of all the creations of Brahma."* Without time as an ingredient, Thoreau's artist *"had made a new system ... a world with full and fair proportions; in which, though the old cities and dynasties had passed away, fairer and more glorious ones had taken their places."* [4]

Living at Walden, Thoreau used neither clock nor calendar, remaining quite independent of conventional time: *"My days were not days of the week, bearing the stamp of any heathen deity, nor were they minced into hours and fretted by the ticking of a clock."* [5] He fished and drank at the stream of time –

> *but while I drink I see the sandy bottom and detect how shallow it is. Its thin current slides away, but eternity remains. I would drink deeper; fish in the sky, whose bottom is pebbly with stars.* [5]

He learned this lesson about time: "*Keep the time, observe the hours of the universe, not of the cars* (the train)." "*A broad margin of leisure,*" he found, "*is as beautiful in a man's life as in a book. ... What are threescore years and ten hurriedly and coarsely lived to moments of divine leisure in which your life is coincident with the life of the universe?*" (4:433)

Henceforth, it would be unnecessary for God to make some mistake to expose time as a delusion. Thoreau did not have to "*avoid himself*" to escape the present. He had no need to invent, destroy, or, Brahma-like, embody time. Time could no longer overwhelm him. He found himself living at one with the life of the universe, in the eternal Now.

NOTES

Introduction: Mysteries and Revelations

1 Joyce Carol Oates, Introduction to Thoreau, *Walden*, paperbound edition, Princeton: Princeton Univ. Press, 1989, ix.

2 Raymond D. Gozzi, *Tropes and Figures: A Psychological Study of David Henry Thoreau*, unpublished doctoral dissertation, 1957, New York University, microfilm. A summary version is Gozzi's essay "A Freudian View of Thoreau" in Gozzi, ed., *Thoreau's Psychology*, 1-18. Two chapters from this thesis are included in *Henry David Thoreau: A Profile*, Walter Harding, ed., 150-187.

3 "Natural History of Massachusetts," *Collected Essays and Poems*, 22.

4 *Walden*, "Economy," 78-79.

5 "The Art of Life: The Scholar's Calling" (1840), *The Dial* 1:175, quoted in Perry Miller, *The Transcendentalists*, Cambridge: Harvard Univ. Press, 1950, 474.

Prologue: A Lovely Lady and a Man-Weathercock

1 Thoreau would expand upon this rowing memory in *A Week on the Concord and Merrimack Rivers* ("Sunday," 46).

2 *Collected Essays and Poems*, 524.

3 Harding, *Days*, 79.

4 Harding, "Thoreau and Eros," 145. Thoreau's early biographer, Franklin B. Sanborn, repeated Emerson's tale for posterity when he wrote that "Sympathy" "professed to lament a 'gentle boy,' but did in fact celebrate, in unaccustomed fashion, the sister of one of his pupils in the school of the two brothers." (*The Life of Henry David Thoreau*, Boston: Houghton Mifflin, 1917, 233.)

5 Lebeaux offers a multifaceted analysis of the "triangle" in *Young Man Thoreau*, Chapter 4.

CHAPTER 1
Facsimile Lockjaw

1 Anonymous letter, Feb. 2, 1842 (published 1877), in Lebeaux, *Young Man Thoreau*, 1977, 168.

2 Lidian Emerson to Lucy Jackson Brown, Jan. 11, 1842, in Lebeaux, *Young Man Thoreau*.

3 *Freud's hypothesis:* Sigmund Freud, *Dora: An Analysis of a Case of Hysteria* (1905), New York: Collier, 1963. Conversion disorder is currently grouped among the somatoform disorders. DSM-IV, section 300.11.

4 *Description of John Thoreau, Senior:* Harding, *Days*, 8. (See Lebeaux, *Young Man Thoreau*, for a nuanced psychological and sociological discussion of the father's personality and effect upon Henry.) *Description of John Thoreau, Junior:* From a recollection written after Henry Thoreau's death by local resident Priscilla Rice Edes, in Harding, *Contemporaries*, 180-81.

5 Lebeaux, *Young Man Thoreau*, 117ff, marshals considerable evidence of the siblings' rivalry over Ellen at this time by examining Thoreau's journal entries and other "writings-out."

6 Thoreau to Isaiah T. Williams, March 14, 1842, *Correspondence*, 66.

7 *Walden*, "Where I Lived, and What I Lived for," 84.

8 Harding (*Days*, 159-62) gives the story of the Walden fire. Lebeaux (*Young Man Thoreau*, 211-13) explores evidence of Thoreau's shame, guilt, denial and subconscious motivation. I discuss the incident more fully in Chapter 7.

9 *Walden*, "Economy," 3.

10 *Walden*, "Where I Lived, and What I Lived for," 90.

11 *Walden*, "Conclusion," 323.

12 *Walden*, "Economy," 19-20.

13 *A Week on the Concord and Merrimack Rivers*, "Monday," 131.

14 *A Week on the Concord and Merrimack Rivers*, "Wednesday," 264.

CHAPTER 2
Post-Traumatic Stress Disorder

1 Additionally, Thoreau's vigilance was sometimes quite literally a willed state of wakefulness which he apparently used as a defense against the recurrent mild-to-moderate narcolepsy to which he was prone, possibly a symptom of tuberculosis. (See Chapter 9.) (Away from home in

1843, for example, it became "a daily triumph just to stay awake," according to biographer Robert Richardson, who adds, "This affliction adds a sly and touching twist to Thoreau's repeated use of wakefulness as a metaphor for consciousness and spiritual life." Robert D. Richardson, *Henry Thoreau: A Life of the Mind*, Berkeley: Univ. of California Press, 1986, 126.) – *Main Street as a gantlet: Walden*, "The Village," 168-69.

2 Thoreau, *Journal Vol. 1: 1837-1844*, 447. This fragmentary entry (Jan. 16, 1843) is not included in the Bradford-Allen edition of the journal.

3 See journal entries for March 7, June 1, August 18, and December 15, 1853. I am grateful to my editor, Randall Conrad, for calling my attention to this episode and its expressions in Thoreau's journal.

4 Boneset is an herb used as a cold remedy and fever-breaker as well as a tonic. With characteristic wordplay, Thoreau appropriates the plant's restorative virtues by including the synonym "thoroughwort," which contains his surname.

CHAPTER 3
A Hallucinated Mountain

1 To H.G.O. Blake, 16 Nov 1857, *Correspondence*, 498. Thoreau, who made twenty real mountain ascents in his lifetime, climbed Mount Wachusett in central Massachusetts in July 1842 – the year his brother died – and a second time in October 1854, two months after the publication of *Walden*. The earlier ascent resulted in Thoreau's essay "A Walk to Wachusett," published in January 1843, the first anniversary of John's death. The climb evidently led Thoreau to associate this particular mountain with his deceased brother, creating rich material for the recurrent hallucination. John is invoked, and indeed identified with Wachusett, in Thoreau's poem "With frontier strength ye stand your ground," which introduces his Wachusett essay (*Collected Essays and Poems*, 42).

2 *Correspondence*, 498.

3 To Mrs. Lucy Brown, March 2, 1842. *Correspondence*, 62.

4 Harding, *Contemporaries*, 180. Harding, *Days*, 135.

5 *The Maine Woods*, 118 and 203.

6 *Correspondence*, 498.

7 *Walden*, "Economy," 17.

8 Walter Harding, ed., *Walden: An Annotated Edition*, 327-29.

CHAPTER 4
The "Rough-Smooth" Dream

1 *A Week on the Concord and Merrimack Rivers*, "Wednesday," 297.

2 Parentheses and punctuation in original.

3 Philip van Doren Stern, ed., *The Annotated Walden*, New York: Clarkson N. Potter, 1970, 202.

4 Although Thoreau earned a modest part of his own living giving public lectures, he did not share Emerson's enthusiasm for the art of rhetoric, nor did he scruple about letting Emerson know it. (Emerson earned a substantial income from his extensive lecture tours.) As Emerson observed in his journal following one exchange: "When I address a large assembly ... I am always apprised what an opportunity is there: not for reading to them, as I do, lively miscellanies, but for painting in fire my thought, and being agitated to agitate. ... Henry Thoreau, with whom I talked of this, last night, does not or will not perceive how natural this is, and only hears the word Art in a sinister sense." (JMN, 6:492-93.)

5 In bipolar Type I disorder, full-fledged manic and major depressive episodes alternate. It commonly begins with depression and is characterized by at least one manic phase during its course. The depressive phase can be an immediate prelude or aftermath of mania, or depression and mania can be separated by months or years. In bipolar Type II disorder, major depression alternates with less extreme mania (known as hypomania). Examples of Thoreau's manic attacks are presented in the next sections of this chapter.

6 Estabrook ("Easterbrooks" or "Eastabrook" to Thoreau) is still the name of a "rocky, rough and swampy" land in Concord that Thoreau came to know and love as intimately as he did Walden Woods. (See Steve Ells, "Henry Thoreau and the Estabrook Country: A Historic and Personal Landscape," *Concord Saunterer*, Fall 1996, 4:70-148). The Old Carlisle Road, too stony and hilly for traffic but good for Thoreau-style walks, leads to the neighboring town of that name.

7 For example, in a remote part of Estabrook in 1847, Thoreau and Emerson viewed the rings around Saturn through a telescope owned by a farmer-astronomer who lived alone there. (Ells, 84.)

8 Gozzi, "Some Aspects of Thoreau's Personality," 161-62.

9 *Correspondence*, 302-03. (Interruption at end of this paragraph in original. The letter continues for another page.)

CHAPTER 5
Seasonal Affective Disorder

1 "The Seasons" is given in Harding, *Days*, 27.
2 *Walden*, "Economy," 41.
3 *Walden*, "Spring," 311.

CHAPTER 6
Mind and Brain

1 The authors described "a distinct behavioral syndrome in which affective response is deepened in the presence of relatively preserved intellectual function" (Waxman and Geschwind 1974, 629). Subsequent studies brought the number of identified traits to about eighteen, among which may be mentioned "circumstantiality" ("loquacious, pedantic; overly detailed") and "viscosity" ("stickiness; tendency to repetition"), overlapping some of the five core traits reviewed in this chapter. See Waxman and Geschwind 1975; Bear and Fedio, 1986.

2 Flaherty, 24. The Geschwind-Waxman wording is: "The tendency toward extensive and, in some cases, compulsive writing" (1974, 629).

3 Quoted in Leo Marx, "The Struggle Over Thoreau," *New York Review of Books*, June 24, 1999.

4 Alan D. Hodder, *Thoreau's Ecstatic Witness*. New Haven: Yale Univ. Press, 2001, 159ff.

5 Thoreau notably counseled: "Chastity is something positive, not negative. It is the virtue of the married especially. All lusts or base pleasures must give place to loftier delights. They who meet as superior beings cannot perform the deeds of inferior ones." *Collected Essays and Poems*, 329. Writing to Blake, he did concede that he spoke from inexperience (*Correspondence*, 288).

6 "Violence creeps into many of his sentences, is evident in the curtness of his judgments; it gave his personality pungency and today helps save many of his moralisms from oblivion – he seems more modern than he is." Gozzi, "Some Aspects of Thoreau's Personality," 154. "*As if it burned him*": Harding, Days, 417.

7 Harding, "Thoreau's Sexuality," 39-40.
8 Flaherty, 28.
9 Flaherty, 29-30.
10 Flaherty, 30.

CHAPTER 7
Mood Imagery: Icarus

1 Leon Edel, *Writing Lives: Principia Biographica*. New York: Norton, 1984, 162. Best known for his award-winning volumes on Henry James, Edel was also the author of *Henry D. Thoreau* (Minneapolis: Univ. of Minnesota Press, 1970) and *Stuff of Sleep and Dreams: Experiments in Literary Psychology* (New York: Harper and Row, 1982).

2 *Collected Essays and Poems*, 593.

3 Henry A. Murray, "Notes on the Icarus Syndrome," 141.

4 *Traits 1-5 and 7*: Henry A. Murray, "American Icarus," 631-38. *Trait 6*: Murray, "Notes," 141.

5 Harding, *Contemporaries*, 95.

6 Quoted in Harding and Meyers, *New Thoreau Handbook*, 185.

7 Thoreau used this rooster image in *Walden* ("Where I Lived...," 84).

8 Thoreau later expanded upon this rowing memory in *A Week on the Concord and Merrimack Rivers* ("Sunday," 46).

9 *Walden*, "Economy," 3.

10 R. W. Emerson, quoted in Harding, *Days*, 333.

11 Hyman, "Henry Thoreau in Our Time," 19.

12 Harding, *Days*, 157-61.

13 Psychologically, it has been further suggested that Thoreau unconsciously wanted to start the fire from hostility toward his community or toward his father (John Thoreau, Sr., was a sometime officer of the town's volunteer firefighters), perhaps in reaction against pressure he felt to assume mature responsibilities since his older brother's death. Lebeaux, notably, argues that the Walden fire served to ensure Thoreau's continuing alienation from his townsmen. It could also have served as "a form of self-punishment, a way of courting both physical and emotional disaster," since Thoreau lingered near the flames until the last moment. Lebeaux, *Young Man Thoreau*, 123-24 and 133n23. At the same time, the episode may be considered a call for help from the son to the fireman father – Icarus losing his wings.

14 "Walking," *Collected Essays and Poems*, 255.

15 Murray, 639.

16 To R. W. Emerson, March 11, 1842, *Correspondence*, 63.

17 *Walden*, "Conclusion," 324.

18 Moldenhauer, "Paradox in *Walden*," 76.

19 Joseph Wood Krutch, *Henry David Thoreau*, New York: Sloane Associates, 1948, 286, quoted in Moldenhauer, 73.

20 Harding, "Thoreau's Sexuality," 27. Harding summarizes this essay in "Afterword to the 1992 Edition," *Days*, 1992

21 Harding, "Thoreau's Sexuality," 25-26.

22 Harding, *Contemporaries*, 79.

23 In the spirit of the leading questions from my two mentors which launched this study, I pose the following query for future researchers. Do the multiple instances of failed mutuality, defensive opposition, withdrawal into solitude, antisocial behavior and misogyny in Thoreau's life comprise sufficient evidence for the diagnosis of an Asperger-spectrum disorder? Solitude was not, to Thoreau, simply a want but a need, which he prioritized over his need for human relationships. Consider the numerous journal passages in which he insists upon the strengths and benefits of keeping remote from human contact while focusing on circumscribed interests. (For example, 4:258; 6:439; 7:46.)

CHAPTER 8
Mood Imagery: Daedalus

1 Thoreau, it should be noted, is not penning an original aphorism here, but rather explicating for himself a poem by Emerson, "The Sphinx," just published in *The Dial* (1841).

2 Within two more paragraphs, Thoreau's journal entry is filled with flights of ideas and streams of associations, demonstrating the close connection between Daedalian and Icarian imagery, and mood swings. (See Chapter 4, "The World-Surrounding Hoop! Faery Rings!")

2 Bertram Lewin, "Obsessional Neuroses," *Psychoanalysis Today: Its Scope and Function*, ed. Sandor Lorand, New York: Covici-Friede, 1933, 226, in Gozzi, *Tropes and Figures*, 113.

3 *Reform Papers*, 108 and 133.

4 Michael West conducts a rewarding study of *Walden's* sand-bank passage in *Transcendental Wordplay: America's Romantic Punsters and the Search for the Language of Nature*, Athens: Ohio University Press, 2000. See esp. 185-89, 196-200, and 445.

5 *Walden*, "Higher Laws," 219.

6 Thoreau's journal sketch, 6:467. (Cf. also 13:125.)

7 *Walden*, "Where I Lived, and What I Lived for," 97-98

8 *Walden*, "Baker Farm," 209.

9 *Daedalus as Divine Architect*: Some medieval cathedrals featured a maze pattern on their paved floors. At the center, the architect was

sometimes portrayed in the person of Daedalus, the builder of the labyrinth. "Since treading the maze was a pilgrimage to Jerusalem in miniature, Daedalus also represents the Divine Architect [God]." (Jill Purce, *The Mystic Spiral: Journey of the Soul*, New York: Thames and Hudson, 1980, 29).

> *Thoreau as literary architect:* Ellery Channing, *Thoreau, The Poet-Naturalist*, Boston: Goodspeed, 1902, 39.

10 *Walden*, "Economy," 47.

11 Anderson, *The Magic Circle of Walden*, 214-15. The whole of Chapter 7 in Anderson's remarkable study discusses circle symbolism in *Walden*.

12 Broderick, "The Movement of Thoreau's Prose," 64, 66.

13 Broderick, 67, 70. *Walden*, "Conclusion," 320. "Walking," *Collected Essays and Poems*, 225-26. Broderick, 64.

14 Douglas R. Hofstadter, *Gödel, Escher, Bach: An Eternal Golden Braid*, New York: Basic Books, Twentieth Anniversary Edition, 1999, pages 10 and P7-P8. Pertinently, Hofstadter views strange loops as the essential matrices of consciousness or self-awareness, "a metaphor for how selfhood originates" (page P7).

15 Sherman Paul, ed., "Introduction," *Walden* and "Civil Disobedience," Boston: Houghton Mifflin, 1960, xxix.

16 Hyman, 33.

17 Purce, *Mystic Spiral*, 29-30.

18 *Walden*, "Spring," 313.

CHAPTER 9
Tuberculosis and Depression

1 Harding, *Days*, 44. I would like to thank Elizabeth Hall Witherell, Editor-in-Chief of *The Writings of Henry D. Thoreau*, for sharing thoughtful comments (March 19, 2004) which gave rise to this chapter.

2 *Days*, 152. *Correspondence*, 133.

3 *Correspondence*, 376.

4 *Days*, 357.

5 *Days*, 464.

6 *Days*, 463.

CHAPTER 10
The "Cuttlefish" Defense

1 Richard Bridgman, *Dark Thoreau,* Lincoln: Univ. of Nebraska Press, 1982, 284.
2 To Calvin H. Greene, Feb. 10, 1856, *Correspondence,* 407.
3 In Harding, *Contemporaries,* 4.
4 *Walden,* "Conclusion," 332-33.
5 Howarth, *Book of Concord,* 26-27.

CHAPTER 11
The "As-If" Personality

1 Deutsch, 262, 263.
2 Harding, *Days,* 8.
3 *Days,* 135. The eulogy, of course, overflows with benignity and lumps together several social-reform "causes" of the time. Not every trait ascribed to John, if true, was imitated by Henry. In particular, Thoreau in spite of his fervent abolitionist commitment never joined any organization in support of the "cause of the slave." And in daily life, he seldom showed much tolerance for the inebriate, the ignorant and depraved.
4 Harding, *Contemporaries,* 62-63.
5 *Contemporaries,* 120.
6 *Contemporaries,* 111.
7 Quoted in F. B. Sanborn, *The Life of Henry David Thoreau,* Boston: Houghton Mifflin, 1917, 341-42.
8 *Contemporaries,* 147.
9 Deutsch, 277.
10 *Contemporaries,* 32, 34.
11 *Contemporaires,* 73, 74.
12 *Contemporaries,* 65.
13 *Days,* xiii.
14 Lebeaux, *Young Man Thoreau,* 5.
15 *Contemporaries,* 64.
16 Sherman Paul, *The Shores of America: Thoreau's Inward Exploration,* Urbana: Univ. of Illinois Press, 1958, 180.
17 Porte, *Emerson in His Journal,* 133-34.
18 Emerson, "Thoreau," 447-48.
19 "Civil Disobedience," ¶ 27, *Reform Papers* 81.

CHAPTER 12
Other Personality Traits

.1 *The Diagnostic and Statistical Manual of Mental Disease*, various editions, Washington DC: American Psychiatric Association.

2 Harding, Foreword to Thoreau, *Journal,* rpt. 1962, Dover, v.

3 Such, at least, is the literal translation. This fragment is usually quoted in a translation popularized by the historian Isaiah Berlin: "The fox knows many little things. The hedgehog knows one big thing." But Berlin triggered a prickly philological disputation that would have pleased Thoreau. Suffice it to say that "trick," not "thing," is a closer rendition, and so the poet's comparison favors the hedgehog, since "(1) the hedgehog's trick is superior to the fox's many tricks, and (2) the hedgehog's trick may actually defeat the fox." The trick, of course, is to roll itself into a ball. (John S. Bowman, letter to the editor, *New York Review of Books*, Sept. 25, 1980. See also Berlin's reply, Oct. 9, 1980.)

4 *Collected Essays and Poems*, 31.

5 Most recently, Alan Hodder refers to *"Walden* as a paradigmatic text or sacred scripture" (*Thoreau's Ecstatic Witness*, xiii.)

6 Rosenwald, 161, 170-71.

7 See Erik Erikson, *Identity: Youth and Crisis*, New York: Norton, 1968, 91-207.

8 *Walden*, "Economy," 4.

9 *Walden*, "Brute Neighbors," 236.

10 *Walden*, "Conclusion," 323.

11 *Walden,* "Where I Lived," 90; "Economy," 3.

12 Nietzsche, a moralist with some kinship to Thoreau, characterized the complementary Dionysian and Apollonian types in his first book. (Friedrich Nietzsche, *The Birth of Tragedy* (1871), Parts 1 and 6, tr. Ian C. Johnston (2000, rev. 2003), Malaspina-University College, Nanaimo, BC, n. p. (online publication).

13 To Isaiah J. Williams, Sept. 8, 1841, *Correspondence*, 52.

14 Oates, "Introduction," Thoreau, *Walden,* 1989 (paperback), xv.

15 Harding, "Thoreau's Sexuality," 41.

16 Thoreau was a "Yankee Diogenes" in *Putnam's Monthly Magazine* in 1854 and an "American Diogenes" in *Chambers's Journal* in 1857. "He may truly be called the 'Diogenes' of the 19th century," Abigail

Alcott wrote in 1848 (Walter Harding, "Thoreau and the Lexington Lyceum," *Thoreau Society Bulletin* 161 [Fall 1982], 2).

17 *Walden,* "Conclusion," 327; "Economy," 17.

18 See esp. Cavell, 16-24.

CHAPTER 13
Battle of the Mind

1 To H.G.O. Blake, Sept. 26, 1859, *Correspondence,* 558.

2 *Walden,* "The Bean Field," 159.

4 *A Week on the Concord and Merrimack Rivers,* "Monday," 126.

5 Thoreau further remarked: "*If I have got false teeth, I trust that I have not got a false conscience. It is safer to employ the dentist than the priest to repair the deficiencies of nature.*"

6 Ellery Channing, *Thoreau: The Poet-Naturalist,* 337.

7 *Walden,* "Sounds," 111.

8 To H.G.O. Blake, Nov. 20, 1849, *Correspondence,* 251. Thoreau's italics.

CHAPTER 14
The Kalendar Project

1 Bradley P. Dean, ed., "Introduction," Thoreau, *Wild Fruits,* New York: Norton, 2000, xi.

For discussions of what is known or conjectured about the final project Thoreau envisioned, see also: Elizabeth Hall Witherell, "Thoreau's Transcendental Natural History," presentation, Concord (Mass.) Museum, Jan. 24, 1999; and Robert D. Richardson, "Introduction," Thoreau, *Faith in a Seed,* ed. B. P. Dean, Washington: Island Press, 1993, 4-11.

2 "Huckleberries," *Collected Essays and Poems,* 501.

3 *Walden,* "Solitude," 138.

4 Porte, "A Purely Sensuous Life," 199.

CHAPTER 15
Writing It Out

1 Sayre, *New Essays,* 5.

2 *Walden,* "Economy," 19-20.

3 Johnson, *Thoreau's Complex Weave,* xi.

4 "Civil Disobedience" is discussed from another perspective in Chapter 11, "Paradigmatic."

5 *A Week on the Concord and Merrimack Rivers,* "Saturday," 19-20.

6 Thoreau, "Paradise (to be) Regained," *Reform Papers,* 47.

7 Carl Hovde discusses the point in "The Conception of Character in *A Week on the Concord and Merrimack Rivers,*" in *A Thoreau Centennial,* Walter Harding, ed., New York: State Univ. Press, 1964, 7.

8 *A Week on the Concord and Merrimack Rivers,* "Monday," 131.

9 *Cape Cod,* 147.

10 Hyman, 28.

11 *Walden,* "Spring," 309, 311. See also Thoreau's letter to R. W. Emerson, March 11, 1842, *Correspondence,* 63, on the death of the latter's young son; and an extended journal meditation around August 1850 (2:43-45).

12 *Walden,* "Spring," 344.

13 "Civil Disobedience," ¶34, *Reform Papers,* 84.

14 Porte, *Emerson and Thoreau,* 35.

15 Harding, *Days,* 205.

16 *Walden,* "Reading," 102.

17 *Walden,* "The Village," 171.

18 "Civil Disobedience," ¶20, *Reform Papers,* 73-74.

CHAPTER 16
A Monarch Surveys

1 *Walden,* "Where I lived," 82. (Thoreau's emphasis.)

Epilogue: A Winged Life and an Artist's Staff

1 *Walden,* "Conclusion," 333.

2 *Walden,*" Economy," 17.

3 *Walden,* "Where I Lived and What I Lived For," 98.

4 *Walden,* "Conclusion," 326-27.

5 *Walden,* "Sounds," 112. Thoreau adds that he *"lived like the Puri Indians, of whom it is said that 'for yesterday, to-day, and to-morrow they have only one word, and they express the variety of meaning by pointing backward for yesterday, forward for to-morrow, and overhead for the passing day.'"*

6 *Walden,* "Where I Lived and What I Lived for," 98.

References

For Thoreau's major writings, I have generally referred to the ongoing, authoritative *Writings of Henry D. Thoreau*. (I have preferred to call Thoreau's "Resistance to Civil Government" by its common title, "Civil Disobedience.")

For the convenience of readers of other editions of *Walden*, "Civil Disobedience," and *A Week on the Concord and Merrimack Rivers*, citations from these works include the chapter title and/or paragraph number in addition to the pagination.

Thoreau's verse and minor prose are cited from the Library of America edition of the *Collected Essays and Poems*.

In the interest of maintaining modernized spellings and punctuation in citations from Thoreau's journal, I refer to the 14-volume 1906 edition by Bradford and Allen, *The Journals of Henry David Thoreau*. The identical pagination is available in the two-volume reprint by Dover Publications (1962) or the 14-volume paperback reprint by Peregrine Smith Books (1984).

By Henry David Thoreau

Cape Cod, Joseph J. Moldenhauer, ed. Princeton: Princeton Univ. Press, 1988.

Collected Essays and Poems, Elizabeth Hall Witherell., ed. New York: Library of America, 2001.

Correspondence of Henry David Thoreau, Carl Bode and Walter Harding, eds. 1958. Westport: Greenwood Press, 1974.

Journal of Henry David Thoreau, 14 vols. Bradford Torrey and Francis Allen, eds. Boston: Houghton Mifflin, 1906. Reprints: Dover, 1962, 2 vols., preface by Walter Harding. Peregrine Smith, 1984, 14 vols. Cited by vol. and p. in the text. Ex.: (1:100).

Journal 1: 1837-1844, ed. Elizabeth Witherell et al. Princeton: Princeton Univ. Press, 1981.

The Maine Woods, Joseph J. Moldenhauer, ed. Princeton: Princeton Univ. Press, 1972.

Reform Papers, Wendell Glick, ed. Princeton: Princeton Univ. Press, 1973.

Walden, J. Lyndon Shanley, ed. Princeton: Princeton Univ. Press, 1971.

Walden: An Annotated Edition, Walter Harding, ed. Boston: Houghton Mifflin, 1995.

A Week on the Concord and Merrimack Rivers, Carl F. Hovde, William L. Howarth, and Elizabeth Witherell, eds. Princeton: Princeton Univ. Press, 1980.

Wild Fruits, Bradley P. Dean, ed. and intro. New York: Norton, 2000.

&

Anderson, Charles R. *The Magic Circle of Walden*. New York: Holt, Rinehart and Winston, 1968.

Bear, David M., and Paul Fedio, "Quantitative Analysis of Interictal Behavior in Temporal Lobe Epilepsy," *Archives of Neurology* 34 (August 1977), 454-67.

Cavell, Stanley. *The Senses of Walden*, New York: Viking, 1972.

Deutsch, Helene. "Some Forms of Emotional Disturbance and Their Relationship to Schizophrenia" (1942*), Neuroses and Character Types: Clinical Psychoanalytic Studies.* London: Hogarth, 1965, 262-81.

Emerson, Ralph Waldo. *Emerson in his Journals*, Joel Porte, ed. Cambridge: Harvard Univ. Press, 1982.

Emerson, Ralph Waldo. *Journals and Miscellaneous Notebooks*, W. H. Gilman et al., eds. 16 vols. Cambridge: Harvard Univ. Press, 1960-. Cited in the text as JMN.

Emerson, Ralph Waldo. "Thoreau," *Lectures and Biographical Sketches.* Boston: Houghton Mifflin, 1904, 419-52.

Flaherty, Alice W. *The Midnight Disease: The Drive to Write, Writer's Block, and the Creative Brain.* Boston, Houghton Mifflin, 2004.

Gozzi, Raymond D. *Tropes and Figures: A Psychological Study of David Henry Thoreau.* Doctoral diss., New York Univ., 1957.

———, ed. *Thoreau's Psychology: Eight Essays*. Lanham: American Univ. Press, 1983. See esp.:
Gozzi, R. D., "A Freudian View of Thoreau," 1-18.
Harding, W., "Thoreau and Eros," 145-64.
Hourihan, P., "Crisis in the Thoreau-Emerson Friendship: The Symbolic Function of 'Civil Disobedience,'" 109-22.

Harding, Walter. *The Days of Henry Thoreau*. 1965. Princeton: Princeton Univ. Press, 1992. (Rpt., with new afterword by the author, of enlarged and corrected ed., Dover, 1982.)

———. "Thoreau's Sexuality," *Journal of Homosexuality* 21:3 (1991), 23-44.

———, ed. *Henry David Thoreau: A Profile.*. New York: Hill and Wang, 1971, 150-187. See esp.:
Gozzi, R.., "Some Aspects of Thoreau's Personality," 150-71.
Gozzi, R., "Mother-Nature," 172-87.
Ives, C., "Thoreau: Nature's Musician," 105-20.
Porte, J., "A Purely Sensuous Life," 199-221.

———, ed. *Thoreau as Seen by his Contemporaries*. 1960. New York: Dover Publications, 1989.

———, and Michael Meyer, eds. *The New Thoreau Handbook*. New York: New York Univ. Press, 1980.

Howarth, William. *The Book of Concord: Thoreau's Life as a Writer*. New York: Viking Press, 1982.

Johnson, Linck C. *Thoreau's Complex Weave: The Writing of A Week on the Concord and Merrimack Rivers*. Charlottesville: Univ. Press of Virginia, 1986.

Lebeaux, Richard. "Thoreau and Civil Disobedience: Some Psychological and Life-Context Dimensions," *Thoreau's World and Ours: A Natural Legacy*, Edmund A. Schofield and Robert C. Baron, eds. Golden, CO: North American Press, 1993, 8-17.

———, *Young Man Thoreau*. Amherst: Univ. of Mass. Press, 1977.

Murray, Henry A. "American Icarus," *Clinical Studies of Personality*, A. Burton and R. E. Harris, eds. New York: Harper and Brothers, 1955, vol. 2, 615-41.

———. "Notes on the Icarus Syndrome," *Folia Psychiatrica, Neurologica et Neurochirurgica* 61:42 (1958), 140-44.

Paul, Sherman, ed. *Thoreau: A Collection of Critical Essays*. Englewood Cliffs: Prentice-Hall, 1962. See esp.:

Hyman, Stanley Edgar. "Henry Thoreau in Our Time," 23-36.

Porte, Joel. *Emerson and Thoreau: Transcendentalists in Conflict.* Middletown: Wesleyan Univ. Press, 1966.

Rosenwald, Lawrence A. "The Theory, Practice, and Influence of Thoreau's Civil Disobedience," *A Historical Guide to Henry David Thoreau,* William E. Cain, ed. New York: Oxford Univ. Press, 2000, 153-79.

Ruland, Richard, ed. *Twentieth Century Interpretations of Walden.* Englewood Cliffs: Prentice-Hall, 1968. See esp.:
Broderick, John C., "The Movement of Thoreau's Prose," 64-72.
Moldenhauer, Joseph J., "Paradox in Walden," 73-84.

Sayre, Robert F., ed., *New Essays on Walden.* New York: Cambridge Univ. Press, 1992.

Sperber, Michael A. "Camus' *The Fall:* The Icarus Complex," *American Imago* 26:3 (1969), 269-80.

————. "Thoreau's Cycles and Psyche," *Provincetown Arts* 16 (2001), 42-44.

————. "Thoreau's Afternoon Walk: Mind and Brain at Walden," *Provincetown Arts* 19 (2004).

————. "Thoreau's Hallucinated Mountain," *Psychoanalytic Review,* in press.

Waxman, Stephen G. , and Norman Geschwind. "Hypergraphia in Temporal Lobe Epilepsy," *Neurology* 24 (July 1974), 629-36.

————. "The Interictal Behavior Syndrome of Temporal Lobe Epilepsy," *Archives of General Psychiatry* 32 (1975), 1580-86.

Index

About the Author

MICHAEL ALLEN SPERBER trained in psychiatry at Harvard Medical School, where he taught for many years. He is currently a psychiatric consultant to the Middlesex, Massachusetts, Sheriff's Department and is a member of the Core Team for Neuropsychiatry and Behavioral Neurology at McLean Hospital. His forthcoming *Cycles and Sphinx* is a collection of essays on abnormal psychology and literature. He and his wife live in Cambridge and Gloucester, Massachusetts.